INSPIRINGIMPROV

Nicholas Ball

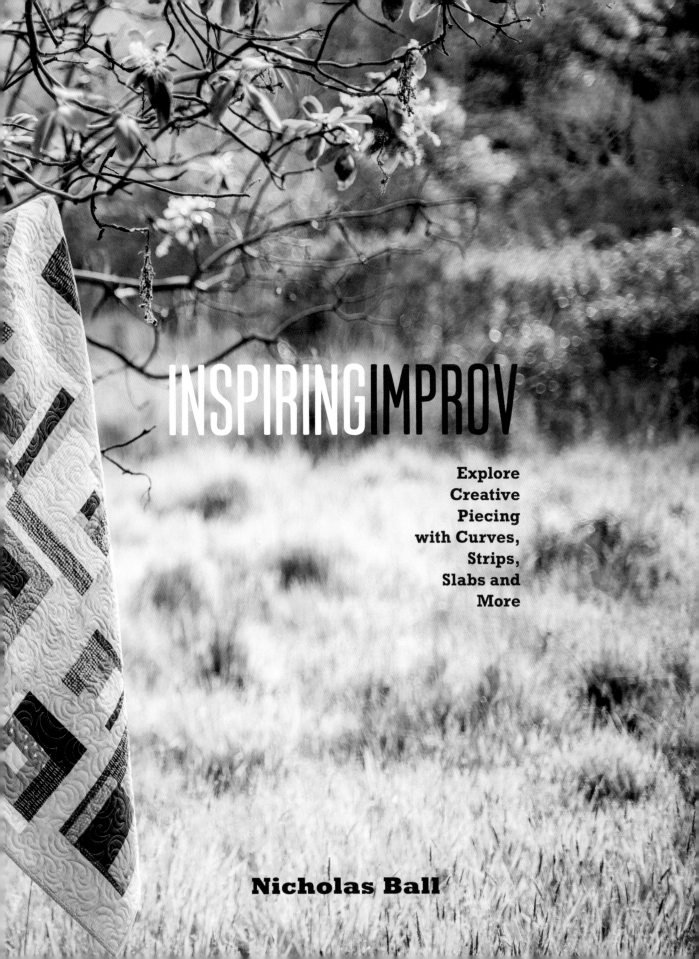

INSPIRINGIMPROV

**Explore
Creative
Piecing
with Curves,
Strips,
Slabs and
More**

Nicholas Ball

Published in 2019
by Lucky Spool Media, LLC

www.luckyspool.com
5424 Sunol Blvd., Suite 10-118
Pleasanton, CA 94566
info@luckyspool.com

Text © Nicholas Ball

Editor: Susanne Woods

Designer: Page + Pixel

Illustrator: Ian Rawle

Photographer: Page + Pixel
(unless otherwise noted)

Photographs on pages 6, 7, 22, 27, 32, 34, 35,
55, 60, & 142 © Lorna Mattocks, Photographs
on pages 23 & 28 © Lauren Hunt, Photograph
on page 25 © Lehua Faulkner, Photograph on
page 62 © Nicholas Ball

9 8 7 6 5 4 3

First Edition

Printed in China

Library of Congress Cataloging-in-Publication
Data available upon request

ISBN 978-1-940655-37-6

LSID0046

For my grandmother,
who taught me
to sew,
to sow,
and the importance
of spelling.

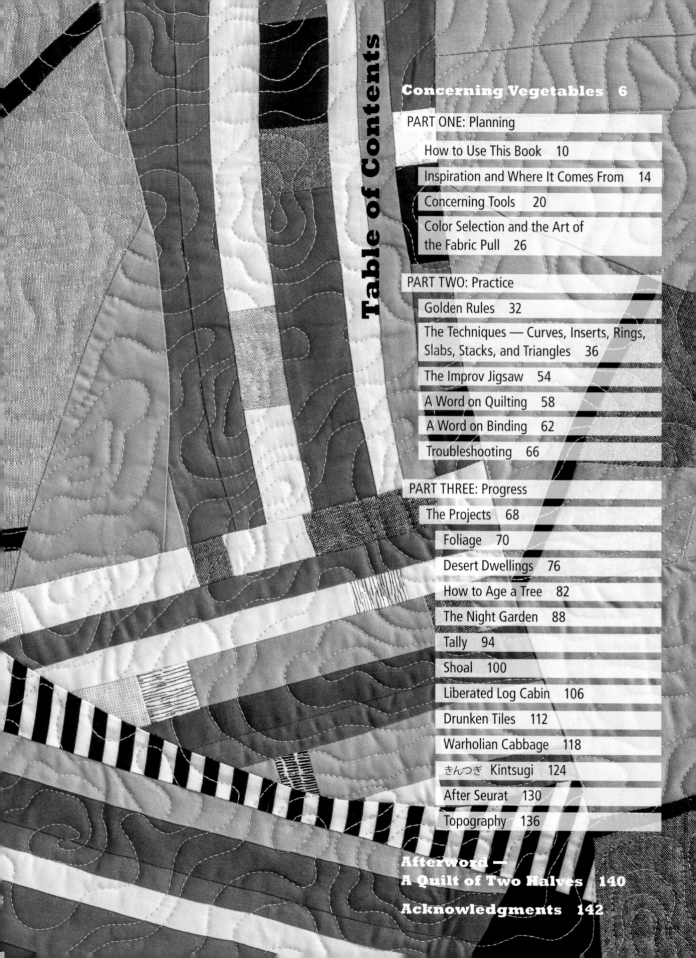

Table of Contents

CONCERNING VEGETABLES

MY EARLIEST sewing memory is of my grandmother teaching me how to thread a needle. I remember being fixated as I watched her manipulate the thread around the needle, squeeze it between thumb and finger and pass it like magic though the impossibly small eye. I still do it the same way. There's a comfort to be had in the familiarity of such a simple act.

Looking back, it's clear that time spent with my grandmother was contributing to my passion for creating. With her knitting bag a permanent feature of the living room and the many framed tapestries that lined the walls, I quickly became enamored with yarns, embroidery threads and the big metal tin filled with buttons. Her sewing machine was set into a table in the spare bedroom.

Though not a quilter herself, she shared the joy that can come from craft and creating with my hands.

Fast forward to 2003 and I'm a photography student with a keen eye for contrast and movement. I purposely blurred my images, cross-processed my negatives and relished experimentation in the darkroom. My photographic approach has always been outside the norm, so it's no surprise that my quilting would take a similar turn. My interest in fabric and fibers was heightened by the textile department's close proximity to our lecture rooms, but it wasn't until 2012, that this interest bore fruit. An inexpensive sewing machine, fabric of questionable quality and the most knobbly thread imaginable combined to create my very first quilt, a slapdash yet valiant effort at half-square triangles.

Making a quilt was always something I'd wanted to do, inspired by seeing quilts on American films and TV shows. Without hanging around to see this maiden effort through to completion, I began my next quilt and then the next. I began to move on from simple quilts and experiment with different shapes, each attempt met with a varying degree of success. Soon, through no fault of the craft, I began to get bored. I didn't want to follow patterns anymore and was eager to push my quilting in the same direction that I'd pushed my photography.

This is where the vegetables come in. When I tell people that my improv journey began with a leek, that's when I get the quizzical eyes and an "are you being serious?" furrowing of the brow. The truth of the matter is that I wouldn't be sitting here, typing away and smiling to myself, if it wasn't for this humble vegetable. I never set out to make a quilt based on vegetables. It kind of just happened. I was flicking through a newspaper

supplement, and there was a recipe for a roasted leek tart, accompanied by a photograph of the vegetable in question. I was so taken by the pattern within. Everything about that leek; the color, the lines and the texture, all of it, was so inspiring.

At that time, I didn't know what improv was. What I did know was that there wouldn't be a pattern for the type of block I wanted to make. It was then that the improv bug bit. Six years later, I'm still scratching that itch. Do I know what improv is now? In some way, I'm still learning; continually changing habits a dozen vegetable blocks later. For me, improv is more than sewing together random bits of fabrics without thought. You can take an idea, an object, or a feeling and translate that into a block or a whole quilt. As a child, my grandmother taught me there's more than one way to thread a needle. The same is true for quilting. Intention is the key. Be confident, be creative, and inspire your own improv.

PLANNING

Part One of this book is all about preparing you for the improvised journey ahead. Whether you're a seasoned quilter or an eager-to-begin newbie, take the time to read through these pages before starting. Here you'll familiarize yourself with how best to use this book, as well as the various tools you'll find helpful along the way. All great quilts start with a great idea, so inspiration and where to find it is discussed, as are hints and tips for choosing fabric for your projects.

HOW TO USE THIS BOOK

HELPING OTHERS TO DEVELOP a passion for improvised sewing is something I thoroughly enjoy. I've traveled far and wide to teach quilters of all ages and backgrounds. Some were staunchly traditional yet embraced the challenges of liberated sewing with enthusiasm and an open mind. With this book, I'll guide you through how I approach improv sewing, from initial inspiration to the tips and techniques used to construct my quilts. Rather than a specific set of instructions that gives cookie-cutter results, *Inspiring Improv* will teach you about the process behind the blocks. With many other titles, readers know what to expect from their purchase. They will make a quilt composed of blocks A, B, and C and, perhaps apart from fabric selection, won't think too much about exploring their own creativity. Using my techniques, no single block will be the same as another quilter's, helping you achieve uniquely individual results without templates or patterns. I want the techniques that follow to serve as kindling for further exploration, igniting an inspirational spark that motivates you to use your new skills and express yourself in ways you never imagined.

The Lack of a Cutting List

Don't be put off by the somewhat vague requirements of the techniques and the quilt projects. I've done away with the specific amounts and long cutting lists of other quilting books and have instead provided "guestimations" for the size and amounts of fabrics needed. If this were a cookery book, it would be full of recipes that state "feel free to add in whatever vegetables you have in your fridge." I love that liberated attitude in the kitchen, and such an approach here allows you to use what you have to hand and not feel like you have to hold off from attempting the techniques. I've always been a fan of jumping in and making things work, so you'll see a lot of "cut rough squares" and "take a large scrap" in my instructions. Embrace this and run with it!

Changing the Scale

With improv quilting, there's no mathematical formula that can be applied to make the units smaller or larger. When sewing a slab, if we want it to be a particular size, we simply stop adding fabric once we reach it. Those slabs can then be sewn into our quilt top or trimmed into smaller pieces. With quilts that don't have a defined block structure, like Warholian Cabbage or How to Age a Tree, the best way to scale them up is to make your starting pieces larger. The approximate measurements within the project instructions will give you a finished quilt size similar to mine. If you want to make a larger cabbage, begin by upscaling the triangles that make up the core. You can then alter everything else to follow suit and the resulting quilt will be all the larger for it. The same applies to all the projects. Like everything else in this book, there are no hard and fast rules, so expect some trial and error. Like Edison's take on genius, improv quilting is about inspiration, perspiration, and experimentation!

{ There are no hard and fast rules, so expect some trial and error.

Implementing the Inspiration

Here is what you will find in every project:

MOOD BOARD

A collection of inspiring images and fabric swatches to set the mood of the quilt.

SIZE

The approximate size the quilt will finish at when the measurements in the instructions are used.

DIFFICULTY

Use these triangles as a guide to the difficulty level of each project:

△ = Perfect for the beginner improv quilter

△▽ = An intermediate project to expand your technique

△▽△ = A little more challenging

INSPIRATION NOTES

The story behind the quilt.

FABRIC NOTES

Information on the fabric I used for the quilt. Use this as a starting point if you want to use a similar color scheme.

MATERIALS

A list of the materials needed to complete the project.

INSTRUCTIONAL TEXT

A step-by-step guide to creating the quilt.

GET INSPIRED

Nifty tricks that make a difference.

QUILTING NOTES

The why and how I made decisions on the quilting.

VARIATIONS

Suggestions on how to vary the fabric, size, and layout of the quilt.

Hexagon Oct

{ **Improv quilting is about inspiration, perspiration, and experimentation!**

INSPIRATION AND WHERE IT COMES FROM

MUCH LIKE THE FABRICS they are made from, the inspiration behind our quilts is often rich and varied. For some quilters, ideas stem from a pattern or a beloved block. With hundreds of layouts possible from dozens of blocks, you can see why this is an attractive starting point. This approach simplifies the design process; the building blocks are already there, you just have to decide how to put them together. As you've probably guessed from the title of this book, I rarely use patterns or traditional blocks in my quilt making, preferring instead to challenge myself to create my own unique designs. As an improv quilter, inspiration is the core of what I do, affecting not only how the quilt is constructed but also the fabrics I choose. This can be clearly seen in my After Seurat quilt, where the artist's paintings inspired the piecing.

{ As an improv quilter, inspiration is the core of what I do.

Sometimes, I'm inspired by something so obscure, I have no choice but to attempt to translate it into fabric entirely from scratch. There isn't a standard type block that will work the way I want. The fact you're reading this tells me that exploring your own creativity in this way is something you're interested in doing too. This gung-ho attitude is a great one to have. It will challenge you creatively and help you to see that inspiration is all around, waiting to be captured. The modern world is a sensory overload, giving us countless opportunities for creative expression. By using this inspiration in our quilt making, the resulting quilts can become more unique and expressive. Where, then, is this inspiration found? Let's take a look at some of my favorite places.

{ **The artist's paintings inspired the piecing.**

TIP: CAPTURING THE INSPIRATION

As you go about your day, take off the blinkers. Look up, look down, look inside and out. Get into the habit of viewing the world with your quilter's eye. When I was at university, we talked a lot about having a photographer's eye: the ability to see and compose images, making best use of the light, angles, and composition. Use this school of thought when looking for inspiration for your quilts. Ask yourself what it is about that tree or feather that holds your attention. Is it the shape, the lines, or the texture? Perhaps it's all three. Be sure to snap a photograph of anything you get inspired by. Smartphones are great because, let's face it, we're never too far from them. Take lots of shots and file them away for future reference. Keep a notebook to hand, so that you can record ideas as they come to you. Look at the source of inspiration and break it down. Sketch out rough shapes and visualize the various sections coming together as a whole. Nothing has to be a fully realized plan at this stage, just a spark of an idea to which you can add further fuel.

Flora and Fauna

It's clear from my Vegetable Patch quilts just how inspired I am by the natural world and the variety of colors and shapes found within it. Vegetables, fruit, and flowers are all brimming with texture and pattern. The animal kingdom, full of feathers, fur, and fins, is a rich and exciting color palette waiting to be explored. Countless curves and organic lines are each a potential starting point for experimental piecing. You don't have to go as far as I did with my vegetable blocks, but next time you're tucking into your lunchtime salad, take a closer look. There may be something there to ignite a creative spark. When you're next captivated by a beautifully shot wildlife documentary, take a moment to look a little closer, past the animal to the shape and lines that make it so enchanting to watch.

The Eclectic and the Everyday

A Victorian cabinet of curiosities, a glittering collection of jewelry and an assortment of geological samples are just some of the more obscure sources that have inspired and informed my quilt making. The allure of the exotic often overshadows the ordinary and can be truly inspiring, yet don't overlook things that are commonplace. Quilts like Tally are born from simplicity. Look to the things you see and use every day, from sewing room notions to stationery, for sparks of inspiration. The simplest ideas are most often the best! As an improv quilter, it's important to change long-established habits early on. Not only those in our sewing techniques, but also when we think about what it is we're going to sew. By altering the way you look at things, you can begin to see the objects not simply for what they are — a

pen, a bookcase, or a postage stamp — but rather as opportunities for creative expression. By zooming in on the everyday, you'll begin to nurture an ability to visualize construction that will push your quilt making out of the box.

New Meets Old

Many quilters believe improv to be a relatively new take on quilt making. They consider the creative abandon with which the quilts are made a sure sign of a modernist movement, with no nod to the past. Whilst it may be true that some of today's improvised quilts hold little resemblance to the traditional quilts our ancestors made, there is most certainly a history of improv to be seen in years past.

Most of us are familiar with the beautifully pieced quilts of the Amish, whose works were attentively hand quilted over the course of many months. Not so well known are the quilts of Gee's Bend; a remote African American community in Alabama. Their collective works moved far beyond traditional quilting boundaries and are a masterclass in improvisation and abstraction. Despite their early twentieth-century origins, the quilts wouldn't look out of place in the Instagram feeds of many of today's modern quilters. Closer to home for me, Wales, which has a strong connection to the quilting traditions of the Amish, has produced similar impressive liberated quilts. Alongside examples of more traditional whole cloth quilts, the Jen Jones Welsh Quilt Centre in Lampeter, houses an impressive collection of improvised quilts, often pieced from oddments of whatever fabric the maker had to hand. Jen's passion and enthusiasm for preservation has given the quilting community the chance to appreciate and take inspiration from these rare and often-overlooked masterpieces.

With a keen eye for line and repeating patterns, the quilts of these pioneering makers are a perfect starting point when looking for inspiring ideas for your own quilts. Look close enough and you'll see that the past can be modern, Avant Garde and forward thinking, just as the present can be the preserve of the traditional.

Architecture

If nature gives us curves to play with, then architecture and buildings give us bold blocks of line and angles. A friend once shared with me something they had learned from a lecturer: that is, we as people spend too much time looking down at our feet or, as is probably more accurate, at a screen. Next time you're walking somewhere, take a glance up. Buildings offer a wealth of graphic shapes and clean lines to incorporate into our quilts. Bricks, windows, pillars, and rooftops offer a geometric smorgasbord of shapes to replicate in fabric. Remember too that the bird's perspective is just as insightful as the worm's. Aerial views, like the one that inspired Topography, work so well as quilts. On my usual route to work I see cracks in paving slabs, paint spills, and road markings, each a potential quilt design to itself. In today's fast-paced, technology-filled world, we often keep our eyes on our phone screens. Slowing down a little and taking it all in will open up your eyes to the inspiration that is waiting for you.

{ Buildings offer a wealth of graphic shapes and clean lines to incorporate into our quilts.

CONCERNING TOOLS

LET ME START by saying that I am not providing an exhaustive list of things I want you to run out and buy. I've never been a fan of being told that I have to have this and that to create successfully. With each new "must have" quilting gadget that comes along, it's easy to get confused between the "needs" and the "wants." What follows are the things I find make my improv sewing that little bit easier. The tools needed to make improv quilts are not unique and you may already have everything you need to get started. If you don't, you can certainly sew away with little consideration for what's listed here.

One thing I will stress is to buy the best you can afford. We've all been tempted by the lure of the bargain bin. In my experience, what seems like a great, money-saving idea usually serves to cost me in time. Cheap threads snap, low-priced blades dull quickly, and patience wears thin. You don't have to spend a fortune but investment in quality now will bear fruit in the long run.

Scissors and Rotary Cutters

There are two types of people in this world. Those who know never to cut anything other than fabric with their best scissors and those who don't. If, like me, you share your house with one of the latter type, be sure to keep your fabric scissors out of sight, or label them in an over-the-top way to avoid any confusion as to their intended purpose. I regularly use scissors to cut fabric before I reach for my rotary cutter. I like to have a large pair to hand for cutting chunks from yardage or to make my own scraps and I keep a smaller pair next to my sewing machine. These are particularly useful for trimming fabric pieces to fit as you're sewing.

There is a lot of hacking and slicing with improv, sometimes through many layers of fabric, and a good quality rotary cutter is a must. I prefer the 45mm size, which I use for all of my cutting. Be sure to have lots of spare blades to hand so that you can change one out as soon as you notice any resistance when cutting.

Tape Measure

Traditionally speaking, I tend not to use measurements in my quilting. That said, a tape measure, particularly a longer one designed for quilters, is a useful addition to the improv toolbox. I use one to quickly get an approximate size of my quilt once the top is pieced, as well as for roughly measuring my backing and batting before cutting to size. When arranging units and making use of negative space, a flexible tape measure is great for quickly calculating an approximate size of fabric that can then be roughly cut with scissors.

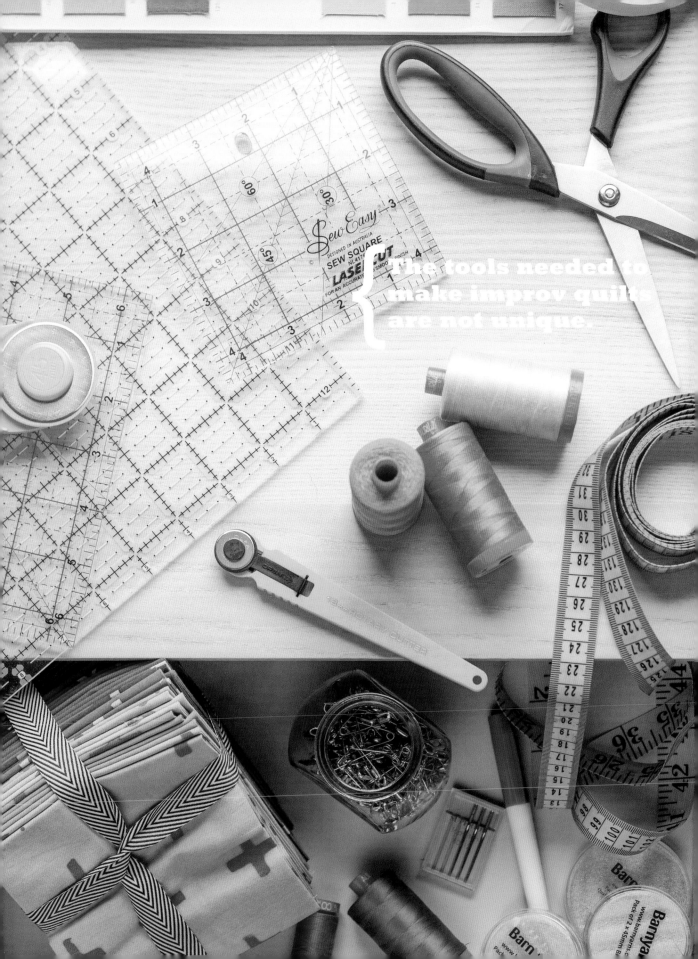

The tools needed to make improv quilts are not unique.

Sewing Machine

A sewing machine is perhaps the most important tool and one that, if you're reading this book, you almost certainly already have. Since I began quilting in 2012, I've had five different machines. Each was a step up from the last in terms of what it could do, chosen for features to make my sewing life easier. Bear in mind that you don't need an all-singing, all-dancing machine to create beautiful quilts. Yes, an automatic thread cutter is a useful thing to have, but it's what you do with a machine that counts. If you are looking to purchase a new machine, my advice would be to buy from a reputable dealer who can help you choose a machine that's right for you.

From a quilting point of view, some things to look for in a machine are the ability to stop with the needle down, variable speed control, and the option to lower the feed dogs. With both a walking foot and a darning foot, you'll be able to vary the quilting you use to finish your quilts, and although I'll go on to stress the unimportance of a quarter-inch seam with some of the techniques of the book, a dedicated quarter-inch foot will ensure accuracy when joining rows and attaching binding. An extension table will give you extra space and steady the fabric when quilting.

Taking the time to look after your machine will keep it happy and humming along for years. Be sure to clean out your bobbin area regularly, removing any accumulated lint. This is particularly important if you use free-motion quilting to finish your quilts, as the high speed and movement of the needle makes a lot of fluff. Oil your machine if required and periodically check that the feed dogs are clean and free from dust. If you're not going to be using your machine for a long period of time, covering it will help keep it in tip-top condition.

Rulers

Many people think that because improv quilts are "wonky," they must be made without the use of a ruler. While I encourage ruler-free cutting throughout this book, a good quality ruler is still handy for cutting binding and for squaring up blocks. I find a 6″ × 24″ ruler to be the most useful size. I use it to cut full width of fabric strips and to straighten up the edges of longer slabs. This size ruler is especially useful when it comes to using the jigsaw method to join improv units together (see page 54). I also have a number of square rulers on hand to help me easily trim units to a uniform size. I mostly use a 6½″ and a 12½″ square, as well as a 1″ × 12″ ruler that is perfect for using to slice into smaller units such as wonky crosses.

Masking Tape

I always have this within reach, particularly the thinner type designed for marking quilting lines. I use it when arranging units on my design wall to see how a particular section will look when sewn together. I manipulate the fabric to match the seam I'm thinking of sewing and hold it in place with tape. It can also be used to mark the perimeter of a sewn section prior to trimming.

Needles

An 80/12 topstitch needle is my go-to for quilting and piecing. If you get the opportunity, try installing a topstitch titanium-coated needle into your machine. They are layered with titanium nitride that makes them last five to eight times longer than conventional needles. If you are using a nickel-plated needle, be sure to change it regularly, either after you complete a quilt or every eight hours if it's a particularly large and complex piece.

Inspiration Board

I always cut away a small swatch of each fabric I am using in my quilt and attach it with a pin to a small corkboard. I also attach any inspirational images that are key to my design and take a photograph of the entire board prior to assembly. It serves as a quick reminder of my quilting goals whenever I need it.

Spray Starch Alternative

This is a staple in my sewing room and something I'm grateful to have been introduced to. It acts like spray starch but is so much better. Together with my enthusiastic pressing, these sprays work to make my improv seams lie beautifully smooth. With improv blocks, you never quite know where your seam lines and fabric bulk will lie. This product ensures my blocks are finished as good as they can be and gets my quilting off to a great start.

Temporary Fabric Adhesive

For me, using spray adhesive is the only way to baste a quilt top and prepare it for quilting. My first encounter with basting pins was not a happy one, though like all the best suspense novels, I'll leave you waiting for the climactic ending until later. From the first time I tried basting spray, I loved its ease of use and the quality of the result. My favorite brand is Odif 505, which is colorless, odorless, and repositionable.

My preferred basting method is to fix the backing to the floor or, if the quilt top is small enough, to my cutting table, with brown packing tape. Then make it as flat and taut as possible. After layering the batting on top, I fold it back, spray a thin layer of fabric adhesive, and smooth it down. I work in halves and repeat for the other side of the batting and then the quilt top. As laborious as it is, pressing your backing well ensures the best success for your quilting. The same is true of the quilt tops, especially ones with many improv seams! I then give the basted quilt a final light press, taking care to avoid any overspray on the extra batting and backing. The quilt can stay basted like this for many weeks and the spray will release once the quilt has been washed, though I have quilts that haven't been washed that show no ill effects from the spray having been left untouched.

Design Wall

Having somewhere to place completed blocks and play with their layout is useful, whatever type of quilt you make. With improv, when there is often a lot of back and forth between the machine and the cutting mat, a design wall can help you see if everything is fitting together nicely. This avoids scrambling around on the floor or running out of table space. While I appreciate not everyone has the room, if you do have a spare bit of wall, you'll find the distance you can put between yourself and quilts in progress is invaluable. You can assess composition, color, and movement face-on and leave the units to stew, as you contemplate the design. A design wall can be as simple as a piece of batting tacked to your wall. A more permanent solution is to cover polystyrene boards or tiles with batting and affix these to the wall. These can then be easily taken down when necessary. I also have a smaller, portable design wall that I find useful for taking units to be sewn over to the sewing machine. I can arrange them as needed and not worry about forgetting what goes where. To keep your design wall in tip-top condition, use a lint roller to remove any stray threads from the batting.

Disappearing Fabric Marker

These are great for giving yourself reference points on your improv units, especially when it comes to piecing those units together. For quilts that don't have a structured, regular-sized layout and for times when you're filling in a background, being able to draw directly on the units and remind yourself of where things should be cut or sewn, is really useful. With quilts like Warholian Cabbage and other intricately pieced examples, in the flurry of arranging the units it's easy to forget what goes where, particularly if you leave the project and come back to it later. A disappearing marker allows you to make "notes" on your fabric without the worry of having to make sure they can't be seen. Just be sure to test on a scrap of fabric before you get too heavy-handed with the ink. Take care when pressing, as many markers can become permanent when set with heat.

Thread

The debate about which thread is best is an age-old one. Many who sew, struggle to balance thriftiness with the need for quality. A sewing friend once told me that not all threads are created equal, and I certainly have experience that testifies to that. The bottom line is that cheap thread does not a happy stitcher make. These aren't spun as tightly as quality, branded thread. The resulting loose fibers can wear at your machine's tension disks, snap easily, and aren't as hardwearing. When you've invested money in your sewing machine and time in your project, it's really not worth taking the chance.

My preferred brand is Aurifil. Recognizable by their bright spools, this Italian-made thread comes in a variety of weights and a rainbow of colors. I use the 50wt for all my piecing and quilting. This medium-weight, cotton thread blends into seams and is perfect for when you want the quilting to add texture, but not see the thread too much. I generally use a light gray or cream for all my piecing and tend to match both the top and bottom threads. For more pronounced quilting, Aurifil's 40wt and 28wt are equally excellent choices.

Thread is a personal preference and I encourage you to experiment to find a brand and type that works for you. Whatever your choice, make sure you have a few extra spools to hand in case of emergencies. Store your thread away from direct sunlight and protect it from dust. Before starting a quilt, take the time to wind several bobbins so that they are easily changed when one runs out. If you tend to use a lot of thread colors in your quilting, a shade card produced by many thread manufacturers is a great way to make sure you get a perfect match. They're also useful for when you need to identify a particular spool that has lost its label.

COLOR SELECTION AND THE ART OF THE FABRIC PULL

FABRIC, fundamentally, is a simple thing, yet is at the heart of what we as quilters do. Of course, making a quilt relies on more than this, but nothing conveys mood and meaning like the rich and varied fabrics we make them from. Think back to the most intricately pieced quilt you've ever made. Now imagine it all in plain white. While the seams would provide interest, would the quilt tell the same story if made in color? Would the play between the piecing be as interesting? Would it evoke the same feelings?

When it comes to choosing fabrics for my quilts, I have a checklist. I want the fabrics to be emotive. I want them to tell a story, individually and as a whole throughout the quilt. I want them to be reflective of the inspiration, but not rigidly so. I want them to unify the individual pieces that make up the quilt into a cohesive finished piece, from background to binding. To achieve this, I use pattern and prints, tone and texture, color and contrast. I combine these elements to enhance the effectiveness of my finished quilt. For quilters who follow a pattern when making a quilt, some are so inspired by what they are making, they hope to replicate it in its entirety and seek out the same fabrics. For others, color choice is much more personal and the fabric pull is an important part of their process.

{ Nothing conveys mood and meaning like the rich and varied fabrics we make them from.

Color Theory and the Color Wheel

With such an abundance of choices, how then should we go about choosing the fabrics for our quilts? While it's natural to look to color theory for guidance, this school of thought covers a multitude of definitions and concepts that use mathematics, chemistry and even physics in an attempt to fully explain the many interpretations of the color wheel. With whole books dedicated to the subject, these pages aren't the place to dissect such theories and I, as someone who has a more spontaneous approach to color, am equally baffled as some of you may be. To keep it simple, consider the following:

WARM AND COOL

The colors, or hues as they are sometimes referred to, that occupy the color wheel can be divided into two main groups. Warm colors, like red and yellow, are stimulating and energetic. Cool colors, like green and blue, are calm and soothing. Always be aware of the temperature of your colors when making fabric selections.

CREATING VALUE

Value refers to how light or dark a color is. Adding black, white or grey to a color will affect the value. If a color is made darker by adding black, this is called a shade. If a color is made lighter by adding white, this is a tint. Adding grey to a color will create a tone. These terms are often easily confused but just remember that they are describing quite a simple process.

My ultimate advice is to make colour work for you. Use the theory as a guide only and don't take it as gospel. Aim for a pleasing selection of light, medium, and dark values and choose fabric and color combinations that simply make you happy. While they may not be in harmony with the color wheel, don't allow that to stop your creative experimentation.

INTERPRETING THE INSPIRATION

All my quilts start off as an inspired idea. We have already looked at where this inspiration comes from, so how do we now translate this into fabric? Some inspiration speaks for itself. Quilts like Foliage, Shoal, and other nature-inspired projects lend themselves to a particular color. We all know that leaves are green and the sea is blue, so we have a starting point. You can use this initial color scheme as a guide when starting to collate fabrics, though don't feel you have to stick rigorously to the palette provided. Yes, leaves are generally green, but there's nowhere that says they can't be pink too. Nature is full of brilliant and unexpected colour combinations.

For quilts with a less specific source of inspiration, I encourage you to explore color in a unique and personal way. Quilts like Drunken Tiles and Liberated Log Cabin are blank canvases waiting for you to fill them with your desired collection of fabrics. Choosing fabrics need not be rocket science. Find an image that you like and use that as a starting point for your fabric pull. Use tools like online palette builders to upload images and find possible solid fabric matches from many manufacturers. You can then raid your stash or fabric store for coordinating prints.

To begin, I encourage you to select everything that catches your eye. Seek out prints with different scales and use them to suggest texture or pattern. Mix angular and geometric shapes with more organic lines. See how your chosen colors and prints play with each other. Do they appear cohesive? This stage is noncommittal and purely experimental; remember, you can always edit down later. To facilitate pulling fabric, I like to separate my prints from my solids, which I then arrange in color order. Aside from my most prized fabrics, which I group by designer, I keep all others in a similar rainbow order. I find this most conducive when collating fabrics for a quilt. The same is true for scraps (and I unashamedly admit to saving every last one) kept in color-coordinated tubs for ease of use. When adding fabrics to your stash, as difficult as it may be, try to make selective purchases. You want to curate a well-rounded stash. As well as solids, look for tone-on-tone prints that often read as solid. Aim for a wide range of values, from highly saturated to the lightest shades. Finally, don't be afraid to move beyond the safety of quilting cottons and experiment with other fabrics to enhance your quilt making. Linens, linen blends, and lightweight denims can add a tactile quality to your projects and be representative of your subject matter.

HITTING A ROADBLOCK

Sometimes, when trying to select fabric for a quilt, we can get frustrated. This is the time to step away. Leave your selection to stew overnight or photograph potential pulls and review them on a screen. This often brings to light certain choices that aren't quite jelling. Check the level of contrast and value by converting the photograph into black and white. Still not happy? Through social media, creative friends are mere clicks away. Reach out and seek opinions!

For those moments when nothing seems right, work within a single fabric collection. This is a great way to achieve a unified look without the guesswork. For collections with several colorways of the same print, choose one fabric and add in some coordinating solids for an instant fabric pull.

Soon enough, you'll have a selection of fabrics ready to be cut into. Before I start a quilt, I like to slice small snippets from my chosen fabrics and pin them to an inspiration board and snap a quick photograph. An inspiration board is particularly useful if there's a specific order you will be piecing your fabrics in, as I did in my How to Age a Tree quilt (see page 82). I also like the idea of being able to look back at past pulls, perhaps reimagining them or adding a new element when I'm seeking color inspiration. When a favorite designer releases a new collection, you can look back at your previous fabric schemes that feature their fabric to add to and create a refreshed pull.

Ultimately, how you choose fabric for your quilts is a choice, which can be as personal and individual as you like. Be prepared for your selection to evolve, trust your intuition, and you'll soon master the subtle art of the fabric pull.

PART TWO
PRACTICE

Practice makes perfect, or so the saying goes — not something that sits well with my style of sewing. Think then of this part as practicing your way to progress rather than to perfection. This is the dive-right-in section of the book: a liberated, learn-on-the-job exploration of a new way of sewing. Be spontaneous and sew with intent!

GOLDEN RULES

IN EVERY PASTIME, from baking to birdwatching, there is a famed, unwritten rule book. Among its "pages" are the commandments of the craft; the instructions deemed to be conducive to success. As amateurs, we abide by them. We daren't be too bold or rebellious lest we get kicked out of the club. Many of you will recognize this feeling of wanting to "do it by the book." For a long time while discovering quilting, I followed these rules like many others. I didn't rock the boat for fear of getting splashed. It worked, for a time, until I began to feel restless, too confined. I needed to get my feet wet, to take a leap into the unknown waters. I held my breath…and jumped.

We shouldn't be scared of taking such leaps of faith. I mean, I'm still here and quilting away! Of course, there are certain rules we must abide by — yet others, which dictate what some quilters see as the correct way to do something, those are there for the breaking. Now, I'm in no way

suggesting that my way is the right way, nor am I disregarding the tried and trusted ways people have quilted for decades. What I want to explore in this chapter is the idea that, as a quilter, doing things your way doesn't make it wrong.

Whenever I travel and teach, I talk to quilters from all backgrounds. I'm intrigued by the various ways we get to the same end. Our destination is a finished quilt, but the speed we travel and the route we take differ greatly. I've learned that there are things I wholeheartedly agree with, while others I actively rebel against. Some of these suggestions may raise a few eyebrows and cause the staunchest traditionalists to mutter under their breath. What follows is only my way of working and is advantageous to an improvised approach. I share it with you in the hope that by freeing yourself of some of these assumptions, your creativity and quilt making will reap the rewards.

Let's take a closer look.

"You must pre-wash all your fabrics before using them."

Simply put, you don't. Yes, fabric manufacturers vary, as do the treatments their fabrics are subjected to before they end up in our stash. There may be certain finishes or sizing applied to lower quality fabrics that would be removed by pre-washing. Fabrics like hand-dyed batiks are prone to bleeding and ruining a quilt, so removing any excess dye from them is probably a good idea. While I'm not saying I would never pre-wash, I like to approach the task on a case-by-case basis. If I'm using good quality fabrics, then the time saved by not pre-washing gives me more time to sew, and that can only be a good thing.

"Press your fabric, trim the selvages, and straighten it up before using it."

For me, this again is a matter of time, something of which I find myself in increasingly short supply. I think I've only once trimmed a selvage from a piece of fabric before I've used it. Now I Just dive in and get cutting. It's not unusual for some of my improv units to have bits of selvage sticking out at the edges during construction, so if yours do too, don't worry. As for pressing, yes, if you're planning on cutting lots of precisely measured pieces, press away. Liberated sewing is all about freedom, so why not start by freeing yourself from the shackles of the iron wherever possible.

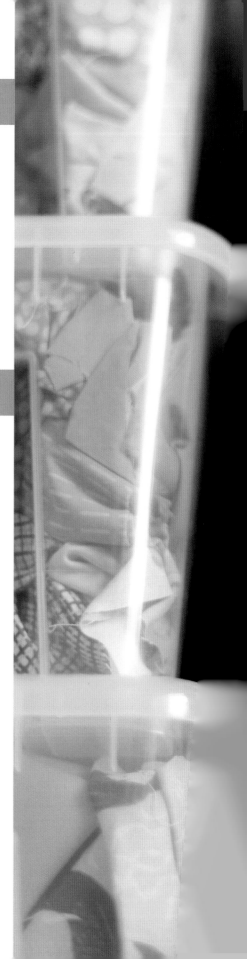

"Always pin your pieces before sewing them."

I can count on one hand the occasions where I have regularly used pins. Actually, scratch that: on one finger. When I'm attaching binding to a quilt, I like to pin it in place around the entire perimeter before I stitch it (see A Word on Binding, page 62). Other than that, pins don't feature heavily in my quilting practice. If there's a seam I particularly would like to match or align, I may reach for the pin cushion, but those occasions are rare. Even when joining rows, I tend to match by eye and don't get too precious about perfection. For some, pins are a safety net. When exploring the techniques in this book, I encourage you to go pin-free when sewing the units. A mismatched seam does not a bad quilt make.

"Join your fabric using an accurate ¼″ seam."

This is considered by many quilters to be *the* golden rule. When I started quilting, I spent such a long time trying to achieve a perfect seam allowance. All the books and all the blogs reiterated the importance of a precise ¼″. I progressed from my needle plate markings on to a masking tape guide before settling on a dedicated ¼″ presser foot. This made a difference and my quilts were all the more exact for it. This precision is a rule I wouldn't break if I made the type of quilts that had an exhaustive cutting list and demanded accuracy. Because these quilts have a predetermined size and have so many seams, inconsistent seam allowances can cause a block or quilt to be too small or too big.

With improv, we've done away with specifics. Usually, we don't know the finished size of the units, let alone the quilt. I'm in no way suggesting that you go to extremes with your seam allowances, but don't fixate too much on accuracy when improv sewing. You'll find that a slight variation in your seam allowance, especially with the curve and slab techniques, actually adds something to the finished unit. What remains important is the integrity of the quilt. You want a solid and stable construction that will last, so while it's no big deal if your seam allowance is off a little at times, be sure to check that your seam is secure at all points.

"Always press, never iron."

I'm a vigorous ironer. There, I said it. I always feel like I'm being watched by hundreds of pairs of shocked eyes when I take my units to the pressing table. I mean, I'm even calling it a "pressing table" and I hardly ever press! I really like to move the iron back and forth, which is great if you want to add a little extra character to your seams. A hot iron can be used to add shape and character to the units you sew and is particularly suited to slabs and curves.

Remember also that some of the smaller units that make up larger pieces of the quilt top, need nothing more than a quick finger press once they are sewn. This is a great time-saver.

These are just some of the "rules" I've encountered during my exploration of quilting, and I'm proud to say I've broken them all. Looking back throughout art history, no stylistic changes came without breaking the rules. Think of the early impressionists, or Mozart. These creatives dared to be different and enriched their fields by being bold. My advice to you as you discover improv, either as a seasoned quilter or as someone new to the craft, is not to get too caught up on the right and wrong way of doing things. First and foremost, you should do what looks and feels best to you. Your quilt, your rules. You may completely disagree with everything I've said here, and that's okay! Just as our quilts are different, our approach to making them varies too.

However, there is one golden rule I never break and that's to have fun. Be individual, experimental, and persistent in finding what makes you a happy quilter. If you enjoy what you're making, however you're making it, then rules don't matter.

{ Your quilt, your rules.

THE TECHNIQUES

AN IMPROV QUILTER'S ARSENAL is rich and varied. In this section, you'll learn six techniques to develop your quilt making and arm yourself with the skills to move beyond the traditional, all inspired by the world around us. For someone who has never attempted liberated sewing before, the following pages may seem daunting at first. There are no specific sizes or set rules, yet however traditional you and your quilting are, the basics are still the foundation. Everything starts with sewing fabric to fabric.

I'm often told by those I teach that the biggest hurdle they face is their own mindset. Their muscles have sewing memory and are rebellious against new ways of flexing. Once you learn to break away from your norm and embrace improv quilting, you'll truly be free to explore your creativity.

Before you think about a full quilt, practice by working your way through my techniques to change your mindset and loosen up those sewing-by-the-rules muscles. Don't spend too much time thinking about fabric at this stage. Use whatever scraps you have as a starting point. The varying degrees of difficulty provide a natural progression, allowing you to feel a sense of accomplishment with each new skill learned. Enjoy this initial exploratory process and don't be afraid to find your own way of working. The instructions that follow are simply guides, and I encourage you to sew in a way most productive to you. Keep everything you produce in practice and review the units often. You may see the seeds of something special, worthy of repeating on a larger scale.

THE FIFTEEN-MINUTE FREE-FOR-ALL CHALLENGE If you're approaching improv for the first time or it's been a while since you've adopted the style, before getting to these techniques I want you to try a liberated, fifteen minutes free-for-all. I recommend using this warm-up before starting a larger project. Take a drink of choice, put on some music, and simply sew scraps together without any thought of color or construction. Sew one piece to another and repeat until the fifteen minutes are up. The spontaneity may surprise you and you could find yourself looking at the beginnings of your next quilt.

Curves

For a long while, my naïve understanding of patchwork seams was that they were straight and strictly sewn with accurate seams. The drunkard's path block, with its sweeping arc, opened my eyes to the design possibilities of curves, possibilities I was eager to explore. The research that followed led to templates, spray starch and an abundance of pins. The tutorial I was to diligently follow talked about "concave and convex edges" and "basting along the scant ¼″ seam." This was uncharted territory. Yet I soldiered on, "distributing fullness" as instructed and trying my very best to achieve the accuracy the block demanded.

That valiant effort was my only attempt at sewing a drunkard's path block. I wasn't happy. My sewing machine wasn't happy as it bore the brunt of my cursing. The blocks were skewed and misshapen, as if drunk themselves. Each was a different size, with no hope of being trimmed into submission.

I've learned a lot about curves in the years since that disastrous first encounter. My exploration of improvised sewing naturally led to further experimentation. I had an idea in my head for a quilt full of color, inspired by the borders of an English country garden. I envisioned a series of blocks composed of strips, each joined to the other by a gentle meandering curve. As we've seen, when inspiration strikes, you run with it! I wanted my curves liberated and made without a pin in sight.

That first experiment opened my eyes to a technique that has become a staple in my quilt making.

PRACTICE

Freehand curves naturally lend themselves to the organic subject matter that I find so inspiring. They are simple to sew, and their versatility means they can be pieced into blocks of any size or used simply to add shape. The curves can be subtle or more obvious and are a great opportunity to break the golden rule of pressing (see page 35). Not for the first time in this book, take the pressing instruction to mean vigorous ironing. An accurate ¼″ seam isn't as important when sewing curved seams. Any variation will only add to the organic nature of the curve. Use pre-cut strips like those in a jelly roll for a fast finish. To add further interest to the curves, consider piecing smaller scraps into the strip before you cut the curve. To do this, begin by making a straight cut in the strip. Next, sew a small scrap to it. Then, press the seam and attach the other piece of the strip to the other side of the scrap.

PIECING CURVES

1. Take 2 pieces of fabric and lay them on your cutting mat, right side up, overlapping the pieces. The deeper the curve you intend to cut, the more the fabric should overlap. (FIG. A)

2. Use a rotary cutter to cut the curve through both pieces and discard the excess fabric. (FIG. B)

3. With the right sides together, align the top edge of the fabrics and sew along the curve. (FIG. C)

GET INSPIRED: When I sew curves, I find it helpful to reduce the stitch length, and anytime you need to stop, make sure your needle is in the down position. You should aim, though, to sew the curve in one smooth motion, sewing slowly. It helps to lift the top fabric up and away from the bottom fabric and guide it into place. Although it might seem like an advantage, resist pinning the pieces together. You want to be able to move them freely.

4. Press the seam using a little steam. I like to press to the side and always in the same direction. (FIG. D) The deeper your curve, the more you'll have to work on the seam. Don't be put off by how it looks in the beginning. Use the tip of your iron to get right up to the stitching and eventually it will lay flat. Trust me!

5. You can now piece the unit into your project (see Foliage, page 70) or continue to add strips until the unit can be trimmed to the block size you need (see The Night Garden, page 88). When adding the next strip of fabric, overlap it and cut the next curve in the same way. If you wish to achieve a certain shape in your piecing, use the previous seam as a guide, or cut freehand for some variation. (FIG. E)

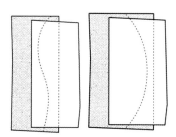

Figure A: Shallow curve & deep curve

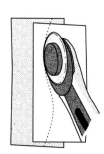

Figure B

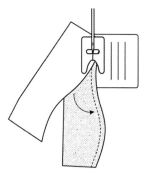

Figure C

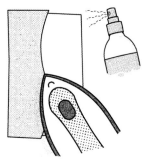

Figure D

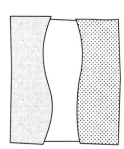

Figure E

Inserts

Whenever I talk about quilting to non-quilters, I usually count the seconds until they ask that trying question we quilters know all too well: "Why do you cut fabric into small pieces, only to sew it back together again?" My answer is often far too rambling and enthusiastic for their liking and the look on their faces belies their gentle nods of understanding. For me, that simple act of cutting opens up a world of possibilities. I'm sure people would be further perplexed to learn that not only do I cut fabric into smaller pieces to sew it back together, I then cut up those pieces too. This insert technique is the epitome of cut, sew, repeat.

I first explored the idea of inserts by way of scrap management. As is often the case, I'd found myself surrounded by scraps and needed a quick and easy way to reduce them. The majority were strips and not quite large enough to go it alone in a quilt. Yes, I could have sewn them all together and made slabs, which, as you'll learn later (see page 44), is a technique equally at home in the improv arsenal. But for this quilt, I wanted something a little more dynamic, something with scale and movement. I wanted the strips to be the star. Like all good performers, they needed a supporting act. I threw in some low-volume background pieces, began slicing with total abandon, and my obsession with wonky crosses was born.

PRACTICE

Fundamentally, one-strip inserts are as simple as it gets: take a piece of fabric, make a cut through it, add the fabric strip in between, and sew it all together. The complexity of the design can be changed by how you make the cuts. You can change the direction, it can be straight or curved, you could make several cuts, crossing over or parallel to each other — the possibilities are endless. The instructions that follow show you how to make a cross unit using two strips that can be adapted for any number of inserts (see Tally, page 94, and Kintsugi, page 124). Be bold with your fabric choices. The insert fabric really stands out when paired with a simple, low-key background. Use an assortment of widths to add further interest to the blocks, either from existing string scraps or by cutting a variety from yardage.

PIECING INSERTS

1. Make a vertical cut through a background piece from one edge of the fabric to the other. (FIG. A)

2. Take a strip of insert fabric and align the long edge with the cut edge of a background piece, right sides together. Make sure to leave a little overhang of insert fabric at each end. Sew the strip to the background fabric. (FIG. B)

3. Press the seam, then sew the other half of the background fabric to the opposite long edge of the insert strip. (FIG. C)

4. Turn the block 90 degrees and make a second vertical cut through the unit in the opposite direction. (FIG. D)

5. Position a second strip of insert fabric along the cut edge of one unit from Step 4, right sides together, and sew. (FIG. E)

6. Sew the other half of the unit from Step 4 to the opposite long edge of the insert strip. Don't worry if the cross doesn't line up exactly. (FIG. F)

7. Press the unit well.

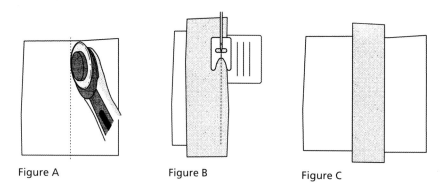

Figure A   Figure B   Figure C

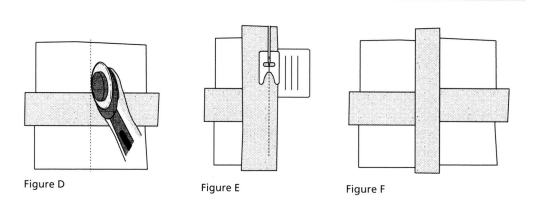

Figure D   Figure E   Figure F

INSERTS: AN ALTERNATIVE CHAIN PIECING METHOD

If you're making a number of units, it's quicker and easier to chain piece them.

1. Make a vertical cut through a background piece. Keep the left-hand piece in front of you and place the right-hand piece to the side. Repeat for all your background pieces. (FIG. G)

2. Trim a strip of insert fabric to size and align it right sides together along the cut edge of a left-hand piece. Repeat for all your background pieces, stacking them and taking care to keep them in the order you cut them. (FIG. H)

3. Take the paired stacks to the sewing machine and chain piece each insert to its background. Once you get to the end, remove the chain from the machine, go back to the start and sew the right-hand pieces to the opposite long edge of the insert strip. (FIG. I)

4. Clip the pieces from the chain and press the seams, keeping them in the order they were sewn.

5. Repeat Steps 1-4 for the second insert.

The chain piecing method can be used for any number of inserts. As long as you keep the pieces in the order that you cut them, you'll have a pile of sewn units organized and ready to go in no time.

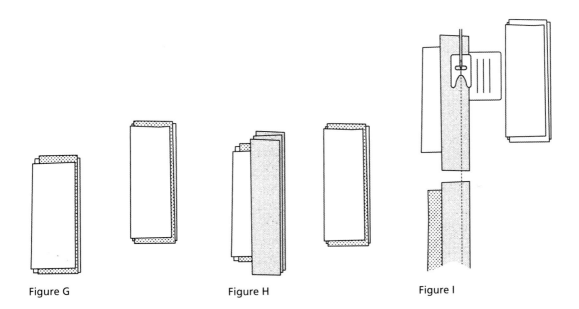

Figure G   Figure H   Figure I

Rings

It's funny to think how one afternoon of sewing would come to shape my entire quilting practice. This ring technique I used to create the leek block in my Vegetable Patch quilt (see page 6) marked the start of a period of creative experimentation that now defines who I am as a quilter. When I made the leek, I wanted the appearance of circular layers without having to use curved piecing.

PRACTICE

The ring technique gives the illusion of curves by cutting lots of angular seams. Change the angle and you change the curve. Next time you cut a leek, take a closer look. At the root end, the layers are near perfect circles. Move closer to the top and they become almost diamond in shape. Use this technique to show not only vegetables, but fruit, cells, trees, planets and more! The number of rings is limited only by fabric and space. Different width rings add scale and interest. Experiment with the starting shape to achieve different results.

PIECING RINGS

1. Using a pencil or erasable fabric marker, draw the shape you want to achieve in the center of a fabric square, making sure there is at least a ¼″ of fabric extending beyond the line in all directions (FIG. A). This shape will act as a guide for cutting and sewing the first round of pieces. The size depends on the scale of your ring unit; the larger this initial shape, the larger the first ring will be.

2. Starting on the right-hand side of the shape, place the ¼″ line of your ruler on the drawn line and trim. (FIG. B)

3. Take a strip of fabric and place it right sides together on top of the square, aligning the edge of the strip with the trimmed edge of the square. Trim the length of the strip, leaving a little fabric extending beyond the top and bottom of the square. (FIG. C)

4. Sew the strip to the square and press the seam towards the strip. (FIG. D)

5. Working in a counter-clockwise direction, align the ¼″ ruler mark on the drawn line of the shape and trim again, this time removing the excess square fabric as well as some of the first strip. (FIG. E)

6. Place another strip along the trimmed edge, sew, and press. (FIGS. F & G)

7. Continue in this way, trimming the center square ¼″ away from the drawn line each time and attaching a strip of fabric until you complete the ring. You will find that as the unit grows, the offcuts from the strips become too short. When this happens simply take a new strip of the fabric and cut it to length as in Step 2. (FIG. H)

8. To begin the second ring, the seams of the first will act as a guide for cutting in the same way as the drawn line did. Again, work in a counter-clockwise direction, beginning with the first seam sewn. (FIG. I)

GET INSPIRED: Either continue to use the ruler's ¼" mark or add variation by using different widths. Just remember to add a ¼" to the chosen width for the seam allowance. For example, to make the first ring finish at ¾" wide, place the ruler's 1" line on the seam and trim. Variation in the width will add interest to the unit and make it more organic. (FIG. I)

9. Sew another fabric strip and press (FIG. J). Continue as before until the ring is completed. (FIG. K)

10. Repeat the trim, sew, and press steps to add successive rings until the unit is the desired size (FIG. L). Rings can be taken to the very edge of the unit, or you can use wider strips of background fabric to make the rings "float" (see How to Age a Tree, page 82).

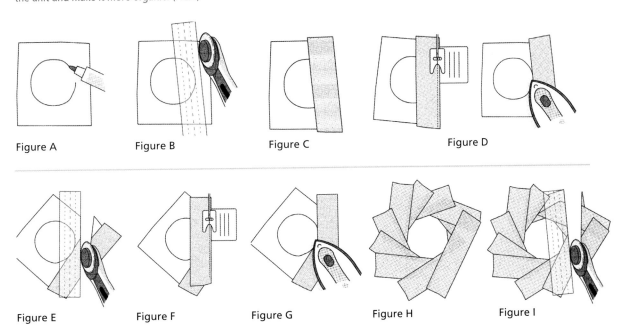

Figure A   Figure B   Figure C   Figure D

Figure E   Figure F   Figure G   Figure H   Figure I

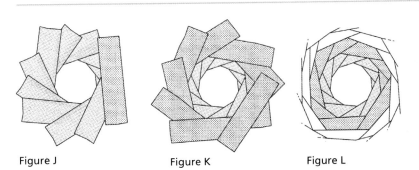

Figure J   Figure K   Figure L

Slabs

Of all the techniques I use in my improvised quilting, I find the slab technique the most liberating. So far, we've looked at how we can take a technique and make a smaller unit to piece into a larger quilt. With this technique, we move beyond blocks and use improv piecing to make slabs of fabric that you can cut and resew in any way you like. They can be trimmed into blocks or hacked into with abandon and sewn back together again. There are no constraints, and the possibilities for creative interpretation are endless.

For those of you who have never attempted improv quilting before, this technique is exactly what you imagine it to be. Take two pieces of fabric and sew them together. Do that a few more times. Sew groups of units together until you reach your required size. Although I'm a firm believer in an "anything goes" attitude, even in improv quilting, you can piece with intention and use the slab technique to create shape, line, and texture.

When working on the cabbage block of my Vegetable Patch quilt (see page 6), I rummaged through my scrap bins in search of something to best convey the organic lines found within. Nothing was grabbing my attention, so I decided to create my own fabric by piecing strips of various widths together until I had a slab large enough to cut up and resew. The texture was there and the resulting block was all the better for having been made so organically.

PRACTICE

The slab technique is great for using what you have. It's a devourer of scraps and works with all shapes: strips, strings, and squares. Using strips presents another opportunity to break the golden rule of pressing (see page 35), and I often attach all the strips first and then press them all in one go, using the heat of the iron to distort some of the seams. A little wave along the seam can add to the look and feel of a block (see Foliage, page 70).

PIECING SLABS

1. Take 2 pieces of fabric and sew them together along one edge. (FIG. A)

2. If you are using strips, continue to add to the unit until it is the required size (FIG. B). If you are using irregularly shaped pieces, place them right sides together and use your rotary cutter and ruler to straighten one edge (FIG. C). Sew and press the seam. (FIG. D)

3. Continue to add pieces to the unit, straightening and pressing as you go (FIG. E). Don't worry about the outer edges of the unit until it is the required size. You can then trim it down to the size of the block you need or cut into it and sew the resulting pieces into your quilt. (FIG. F)

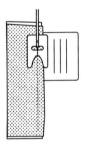

Figure A

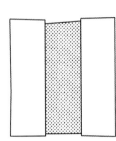

Figure B

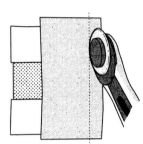

Figure C

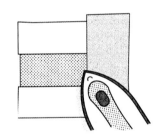

Figure D

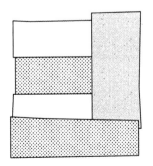

Figure E

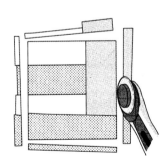

Figure F

Stacks

Patience and perfection are things that I strive for. For me, the two go hand in hand; taking the time to do something will inevitablly yield better results. What I often find myself at odds with is the idea of perfection within improv sewing. How can something so spontaneous be perfect? Yet my idea of perfection is not beautifully matched seams or precise points. It's looking at something I've sewn and, without any hesitation or second-guessing, knowing that it's finished, that it's as good as it can be; that it's perfect. This perfection comes with time and is something I've had to train myself to recognize. But sometimes we don't have time. We want a quick fix, a speedy solution to that last-minute gift we need. The stack technique is a product of that necessity.

There's nothing ground-breaking about this one, yet it remains a firm favorite thanks to its ease and versatility. The idea of stacks first came to me when I was removing the selvages from some fabric (an arduous task I no longer take the time to do). The process was sped up by layering the fat quarters and stripping them of their selvages in one slice. I got to thinking that this five-for-the-price-of-one approach could be used to create lots of units quickly. The sketch pad came out, some quilt math reared its ugly head (an attempt to try to evenly distribute the various prints), and before long I was staring at the primitive origins of my Drunken Tiles quilt. This pattern would go on to be my first publication, so it seems only right that a new-and-improved version should be featured in this book.

PRACTICE

The stack technique is great for putting an improv spin on traditional blocks, like the four-patch, nine-patch, and log cabin. The fundamentals of the technique involve making cuts through layered fabric and rearranging the order before you sew them together. Made this way, the blocks have an originality that may be lacking in traditional blocks. You can alter the angle of the cuts and the fabric in the layers to make a crop of unique units to mix and match in your quilt making.

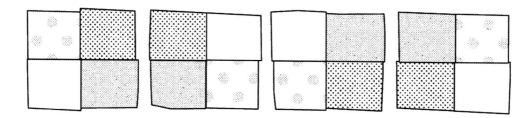

STACKS: PIECING A SIMPLE 4-PATCH

For this type of unit, begin with four large square or rectangular pieces of fabric, all roughly the same size. They need not be perfectly cut, so long as they can be stacked without any one being dramatically larger than the others. If you have a charm pack on hand, this would work perfectly.

1. Layer four pieces of fabric on top of each other, right sides up. (FIG. A)

2. Using your rotary cutter and ruler (though these cuts don't necessarily have to be straight), make a vertical cut through all the layers. (FIG. B)

3. Take the topmost piece of the right-hand stack and move it to the bottom. (FIG. C)

4. Chain piece all the newly paired halves back together and press the seams, taking care to keep the pieces in the order they were cut. (FIG. D)

5. Place the stack back on your cutting mat and make another cut, this time in the opposite direction to the first. (FIG. E)

6. Take the top two pieces of the right-hand stack and move them to the bottom.

Sew the newly paired pieces back together and press (FIG. F). Don't be too fussy about matching the seams at this stage as any mismatching will add to the look of the unit.

Use the stack technique as the basis for further experimentation. The stacks can contain any number of fabrics and they can be cut any number of times.

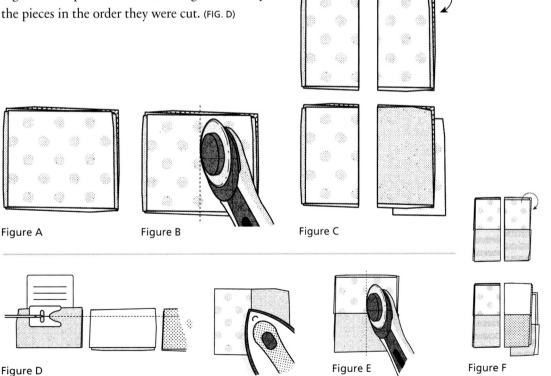

Figure A   Figure B   Figure C

Figure D   Figure E   Figure F

STACKS: PIECING A 9-PATCH

1. Layer nine pieces of fabric on top of each other, right sides up. (FIG. A)

2. Referring to the 4-Patch instructions (see page 47), make two vertical cuts, reorder the stacks, and sew them back together. (FIG. B)

3. Make another two cuts at right angles to the previous cuts from Step 2 (FIG. C). Reorder the stacks again and sew them back together. (FIG. D)

GET INSPIRED: This method yields nine 9-Patch blocks quickly and easily. Now, I'm sure there is a mathematical formula to determine how many layers to move and from where in order to evenly distribute the fabrics, but instead, I suggest that you have fun mixing the pieces until you find a combination that you like. It's not the end of the world if a certain fabric appears twice in the block. Use it as an opportunity to piece the same fabrics next to each other in the quilt to create secondary shapes and areas of negative space.

Figure A

Figure B

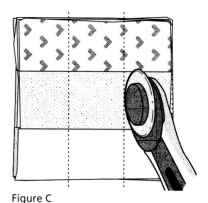

Figure C

Figure D

STACKS: PIECING A LOG CABIN

The stack technique can also be adapted to effortlessly make diverse log cabin blocks.

1. Begin by stacking as many fabrics as you want logs, remembering to count your centre. For example, if you want to make a block that finishes at roughly 10″ square and want your logs to finish at approximately 2″, you will need 9 logs, so you will layer 9 fabrics.

2. Working from the outer edges towards the center, cut through the stack to create piles of individual log strips. (FIG. A)

3. Change the order of the stacks before sewing each block back together, one at a time. (FIG. B)

4. Trim the blocks to size or use as starter units for adding more strips.

GET INSPIRED: A great way to add further interest to your log cabins is to blind pull strips from a bag and add them without overthinking their position. Variation is key. Alternately, consider using an improv HST (see page 53) as the center of your block.

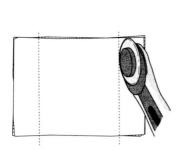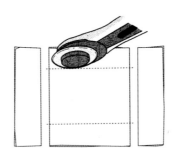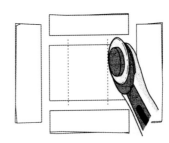

Figure A

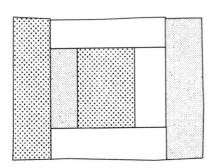

Figure B

Triangles

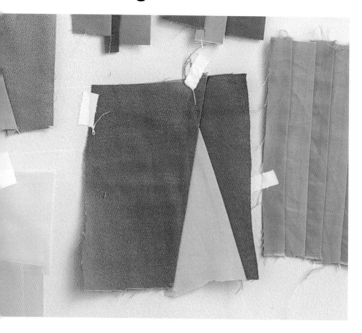

Say "triangle" to most quilters and they'll probably think of half-square triangles, or HSTs. This ubiquitous block can be found in the earliest quilts and is as much a part of the history of quilting as the Amish and English paper piecing. The 1718 coverlet is the oldest piece of British patchwork in the collection of the Quilter's Guild, and it is our most iconic historical example of half-square triangles. Pinwheels, flying geese, and chevrons, among many others, all originate from the simple HST block that remains a firm favorite among quilters to this day.

Like so many others, half-square triangles were the first blocks I ever attempted. My initial foray into quilting was scuppered by many things, but none took away from the creative intrigue these blocks presented. I have no doubt that the endless arrangements possible with HSTs was the first of many lures that got me hooked on quilting. Since those early days of exploration, my relationship with triangles has moved to a more organic place.

PRACTICE

As with many of the traditional blocks in this section, I've adapted triangles to work for you in a more improvisational way. Still the same sharp points and endless design possibilities, but no precise measuring or matching. These units shift and change owing to whatever inspirational source has spurred their creation. Tepees, shark teeth, and cathedral windows—inspired ideas from a simple shape. Another technique suited to scraps, the triangles are formed by combining a square of fabric, trimmed into shape, with larger rectangles that make up the background. When trimming the background after sewing the first side of the triangle, keep any larger offcuts. These can be used as triangles for further units.

PIECING TRIANGLES

1. Take a square and trim two sides to make a triangle (FIG. A). You may prefer to do this in batches rather than finish one unit at a time. Be sure to add variety to the triangles. Cut some tall and narrow and others short and wide.

2. Position a rectangle of background fabric on your cutting mat, right side up, and place the triangle on top, right side up, aligning the bottom edge and ensuring there is at least ½" of background fabric above the tip of the triangle. (FIG. B)

3. Place your ruler along the right side of the triangle and cut the background fabric. (FIG. C)

4. With the right sides together, align the edge of the triangle with the trimmed edge of the right background piece. Sew and press towards the background fabric. (FIG. D)

5. Overlap the triangle and the remaining background fabric on your cutting mat. Place your ruler along the left edge of the triangle and trim the background fabric in line with this edge. (FIG. E, SEE PAGE 52)

TIP: If you're using a solid fabric, you can trim the excess background fabric from the sewn side of the triangle and flip the remaining background piece without cutting it to fit.

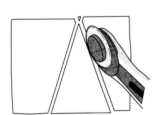

Figure A

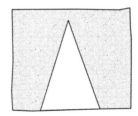

Figure B

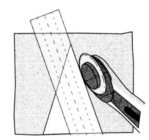

Figure C

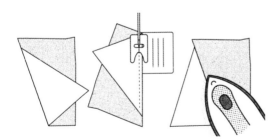

Figure D

6. With right sides togther, align the other edge of the triangle with the trimmed edge of the left background piece. Sew and press towards the background fabric. You now have one completed triangle unit. Do not trim the unit at this stage. (FIGS. F & G)

7. Repeat to complete a variety of triangle units. The units can be joined into rows by straightening the short edges and sewing them together. These larger blocks can be trimmed to size or pieced together using the jigsaw method (see page 54). (FIG. H)

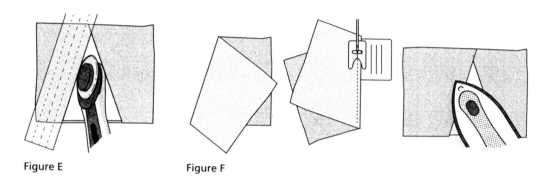

Figure E

Figure F

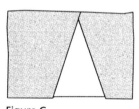

Figure G

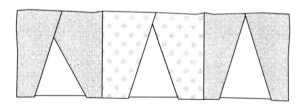

Figure H

PIECING SIMPLE HALF-SQUARE TRIANGLES

1. Place two square scraps right sides together. These pieces needn't be perfectly square or even exactly the same. Repeat until you have a large number of paired squares.

2. Take a pair of squares and either draw or imagine a line running from corner to corner, then join the squares by sewing ¼" to the left of this line. (FIG. A)

3. Take the next pair of squares and repeat, chain piecing until all the pairs are joined. (FIG.B)

4. Remove the chain from the machine, go back to the first pair and sew again, this time ¼" to the right of the line. (FIG. C)

5. Once all the pairs are joined, clip them from the chain, then trim each unit in half along the marked line before pressing open (FIG. D). The units can then be trimmed square and joined together freely or used as the starting squares for making log cabin blocks (see Liberated Log Cabin, page 106).

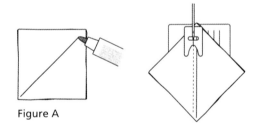

Figure A

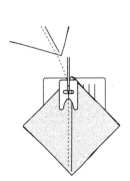

Figure B

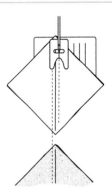

Figure C

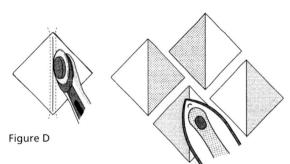

Figure D

THE IMPROV JIGSAW

MANY OF US HAVE MEMORIES
of jigsaw puzzles, either as children or, if you're anything
like me, as a way of making those Saturday nights-in even
more exciting. An ever-present teacher during my youth,
my grandmother first taught me the best way to get all of
those little bits of card to fit together. First, we'd gather all
the edge pieces. Next came the middle. We'd make piles
of like-colored pieces, before beavering away on small
sections. She'd take the roof; perhaps I'd take the flower
bed that bloomed at the base of the cottage. Hours
passed blissfully until the puzzle was perfect, with
each piece nestled neatly into its neighbor. Fast
forward some twenty-five years and I'm still doing
jigsaws. Nowadays they're mostly made of fabric.

Improv is like putting together a giant
jigsaw puzzle. Whenever I teach improv
sewing, I tell my students that first and
foremost they should enjoy the process,
get lost in the moment and create without
any pre-planning. At some point, though,
you'll be at your sewing table, staring at
a pile of pieced blocks. These are your
jigsaw pieces, only this time, there's no
picture to guide you. So what's next?

The good news is that despite being pieced
in an improv way, there are some quilts
that need little more than to square up the
blocks, sew them into rows and finish the
top (see Foliage, page 70, and Kintsugi,
page 124). This is familiar territory for those
of us who are familiar with traditional
piecing and settings. There's always a
picture. Improv does away with all that. It's
like a jigsaw you scored at a thrift store; all
the pieces are there, it's just missing the box.

I love the challenge of sewing different
sized improv blocks together into quilt
tops. Perhaps the most important thing is
to approach the task with an unwavering
acceptance of change. The quilt will evolve
as you assemble it. Blocks will become
smaller, some will be added to and others
will be discarded completely. This is the
evolutionary process of improv quilting.
The quilt will take on a life of its own. It
will dictate, and while you will have some
idea about the finished design, however
vague, prepare yourself for surprises.

How then do we best approach the task
of sewing the blocks together? First, I
use the word "block" loosely. I like to
think of the sewn pieces as units, which
come together in an organic way. As
you make them, leave the squaring up
until the end. With traditional quilting,
once a block is complete, it's often at its
finished size or is trimmed then. With
many improv techniques, as you don't
yet know where each piece will go, it's
best to give yourself as much fabric to
play with as possible. Once you're done
making the units, a design wall or large
floor is a great help when laying out the
foundations of the quilt. At this stage,
you can start to think about the finished
size you'd like to achieve. Mark out a
rough size using masking tape or ribbon.
Take some of your units and use them
like the edge pieces of a jigsaw, creating
a perimeter that you can then fill in.

{ **Improv is like putting together a giant jigsaw puzzle.**

Assembling the Jigsaw

1. Begin by placing units into the space you've created (FIG. A). At this stage you may either need more units to fill the space or scale down the size of your quilt top, so be prepared to make more (or a lot more if you have a tendency to underestimate the amount you'll need, like I do).

2. Look for groupings, units that seem to fit together (FIG. B). While you may not have your jigsaw's box, there are other things that can make the task easier. The ubiquitous smart phone is perfect for recording your layout as it evolves.

As you add and remove units, it's a good idea to take a photograph so that you always have something to look back on should your design be disturbed by a gust of wind or an inquisitive pet.

3. Once you have a small group arranged, use your rotary cutter and ruler to give yourself a straight edge, only straightening the side that you will be sewing. (FIG. C)

4. Aligning the straightened edges, place the units right side together and sew (FIG. D). Don't worry about the other sides aligning at this stage.

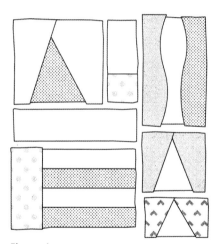

Figure A

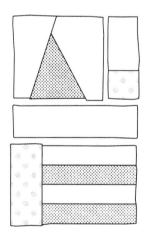

Figure B

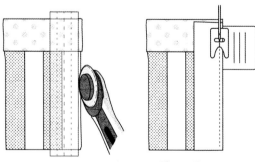

Figure C   Figure D

5. Repeat trimming, sewing and pressing until the group of units from Step 3 is now one piece. The resulting larger blocks are now easier to fit together than hundreds of smaller ones, and you've reduced your 500-piece jigsaw puzzle to a 45-piece one! As the unit grows, change your pressing technique to suit the seam. Sometimes pressing to the side is sufficient, but in areas where lots of seams intersect, pressing them open will help these densely populated areas of the quilt top lay flat.

As you continue in this way, making the groupings larger and larger, you'll eventually be left with only two pieces that will be joined by one final seam.

GET INSPIRED: My grandmother has offered up many pearls of wisdom during our shared years. It seems like her approach to jigsaws was the right one and something that I'm applying to my quilt making today: first come the edges, then the middle, taking all the smaller bits and relishing in the joy as the puzzle pieces are reduced to a single quilt top.

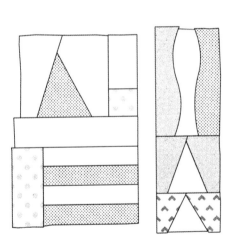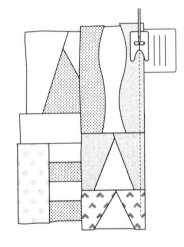

Figure D

A WORD ON QUILTING

THE FIRST QUILT I EVER QUILTED was the second I'd made. It remained nothing more than a top for weeks, so nervous was I of ruining it. The quilt, a collaborative project made over many months with my mother, was a Christmas appliqué sampler, full of charming scenes of Father Christmas, elves, snowmen, and reindeer. We'd chosen the fabrics, cut out the pieces, fused them to the background, and joined the blocks. My meticulous research into basting led to pins, which I purchased in abundance lest I ran out mid-quilt. We spent a whole afternoon scrambling around on all fours fixing the layers together, painstakingly placing the pins "in a grid-like fashion" as the tutorial instructed. With my quilting career still in its infancy, I was not yet confident enough to question and pushed aside such thoughts as "there must be an easier was to do this!" After some hours, with a nagging in our knees, we stood triumphant. The job was done! Next came the quilting, the part I was dreading.

Back then, I was a diligent student. The books I was learning from spoke of in-the-ditch quilting as the go-to, so it was natural for me to assume that this is what the Christmas quilt needed. I readied the sewing machine, attached the walking foot, and, with my tongue stuck out in concentration, started to quilt. Quilting has an insatiable appetite for time and soon many hours had ticked by. I'd finished the task I'd been avoiding for so long, only to suddenly feel a crushing weight of disappointment. There were puckers all over the back. I was so engrossed in the front, I'd not thought to turn the quilt over and see how the quilting was progressing. I was devastated.

Looking back, I can see that a king-size quilt probably wasn't the best choice for my first quilting experience. That aside, I decided then that I'd do everything possible to never have this happen again. From pins I progressed to temporary basting spray, the praises of which I can't sing highly enough. I came to appreciate a heavily quilted look, dense and full of texture. My eyes were opened to the world of free-motion and a new obsession took hold. What was once my least favorite part of quilting soon became much-loved and something to look forward to.

{ Next came the quilting...

There are many great books and tutorials on the subject of quilting that I daren't try to improve upon here. What follows isn't written to teach you how to quilt, but rather to show you how to extend your inspiration beyond piecing and into your quilting. I don't see quilting simply as a means to an end, something to just hold the layers together. For me, its job is to exceed and enhance. I love creating a relationship between the piecing and the quilting and encourage you to do the same, with contrast, density, and texture.

Sometimes, a quilt needs nothing more than simple lines. When I made my first Vegetable Patch quilt, I knew I wanted the quilting to enhance the piecing rather than distract from it. A dense covering of matchstick quilting conveyed the texture found within the subject matter and unified the blocks. Matchstick quilting is a great all-rounder and perfect for all sorts of quilts. The lines don't have to be straight either. Use your walking foot to add meandering curves from one edge of the quilt to the other, like the rise and

fall of the tide or the patterns of a sand dune. If your piecing is linear, this technique is a great way to emphasize that. Experiment with quilting against the grain—that is, if you have lots of vertical shapes in your piecing, use the quilting to add contrasting horizontal or diagonal interest.

If I'm quilting a quilt myself, an edge-to-edge design is my usual go-to, be it with my walking foot or with free-motion quilting. The possibilities for creative expression presented by free-motion quilting are something I would wholeheartedly encourage you to explore. Much like my first foray into the act of quilting, it took me a long time to build up the confidence to take to the quilt top with such feverish sewing.

GET INSPIRED: Take the time to look at your piecing and sketch out ideas. A good idea is to photograph finished quilt tops front on and then print off several copies. You can then doodle away and see how various designs play out. You may want to complement your piecing or provide contrast with different shapes.

I like to take a close look at the inspiration behind my quilts to find a theme for my free-motion. Try to replicate the various textures and patterns to bring a cohesiveness to the work. Dense stippling, echoing, and tight swirls all work well for organic subject matter, while the sharp lines of angular meandering complement more graphic inspirations. If quilting an allover design, I always aim to end the quilting on the excess batting before my bobbin runs out. That way, I save myself the tedious task of sewing in the thread ends. This competitive game between me and my machine sometimes ends in victory and sometimes in defeat. When you have to stop in the middle of the quilt, be sure to secure the stitching so that all your hard work isn't inadventantly undone further down the line.

Sometimes I employ the services of a long-arm quilter with whom I work closely, to create a collaborative vision. This isn't an everyday occurrence, because I enjoy quilting as many of my quilts as possible. Yet for those that require something special, a shared vision really helps to bring the quilt to life. If you use a long-arm quilter, take the time to discuss your ideas. As well as meeting your individual requirements, through their experience, they will offer up their own thoughts about the quilting and perhaps make suggestions that you haven't thought of. A shared understanding of the quilt vision is a great springboard for ideas, expanding creativity in ways you can't when working in solitude. Each quilter works slightly differently and the long-armer you choose will have specific instructions on how they'd like you to prepare the quilt for quilting. This usually involves staystitching around the perimeter and, if you're providing the backing and batting, ensuring it's at least 4″ wider and 4″ longer than the quilt top.

Whichever way you decide to quilt your quilts, I encourage you to step away from your comfortable zone. By reading this book, you've already shown an interest in the unconventional and a willingness to try something new. Take that attitude with you into your quilting and explore your creativity in fresh and exciting ways.

A WORD ON BINDING

MAKING QUILTS is all about preference. Many quilters like the bright and saturated, while others prefer the calm of neutrals. Hand quilting is the only option for some, whereas the look and feel of a densely machine-quilted quilt is the go-to for others. From fabric to thread, batting to pre-washing, our quilting choices are as varied as the quilts we make. In the years that I've been quilting, I've made many choices. Some turned out to be right, others not so much. It is only by encountering these options and experimenting that we find what we like and what works for us.

Of all the stages of quilt making, binding is perhaps my most favorite. This often comes as a surprise to some quilters I talk to, who tell me that binding is the step they would avoid if they could. For me, I enjoy the approaching completion of a quilt I've been working on for many weeks or months. I've worked my way through many choices to find a binding method that not only works, but one I actually look forward to using.

Whenever and wherever I teach, my students are encouraged to ask questions in the final minutes of the class. One question that comes up again and again is: How do you bind your quilts? I've always wanted to write a tutorial on my method, yet time or space has never quite allowed it. I'm happy I get to share it with you now and hope that next time you're finishing a quilt, you'll give it a go. I must add that this is my preferred process and is not the only way.

Even on the rare occasions a quilt may have a jagged or unusual edge (in which case a bias binding may be easier) I use a straight-cut, double-fold binding for all my quilts. It's quick and simple to make and is particularly hard-wearing. Don't be put off by the quick calculation that appears in the first step. This is one of the few times I use any mathematics in my quilt making, to avoid being wasteful if nothing else. I prefer the look of a narrow binding on the back of my quilts, so I cut my strips 2″ wide. Feel free to make yours 2¼″ or 2½″ if your preference is for a wider finish.

TO CALCULATE HOW MANY STRIPS TO CUT AND HOW MUCH FABRIC YOU'LL NEED, USE THE FOLLOWING CALCULATION.

Add up the lengths of the edges of your quilt, then add another 10″. Divide this number by the width of your binding fabric. Round this result up. This is how many strips to cut.

Perimeter of quilt top + 10	=	XX
XX ÷ width of binding fabric	=	How many strips to cut (round up if necessary)
Multiply the strip number by the width of your binding strips	=	Total fabric needed

FOR EXAMPLE

If your quilt is 60″ square, and your binding fabric is 44″ wide:

60 × 4 = 240

240 + 10 = 250

250 ÷ 44 = 5.68, so 6 strips in total

If your strips are 2″ wide:

6 × 2 = 12, so you'll need 12″ × WOF of your binding fabric

1. Fold your fabric along the long edge and align with a horizontal line on the cutting mat. Straighten the left edge, then cut the required number of strips from your fabric. Remove the selvages by cutting across all the strips at once. (FIG. A)

2. Sew your strips end-to-end, right sides together, taking care to orientate them all the same way if the fabric is directional. (FIG. B)

3. With the wrong sides together, carefully press the strip in half, lengthwise, without distorting it. (FIG. C)

4. Leaving a tail of approximately 8″ unsewn and using the largest stitch length, baste approximately ⅛″ along the length of the raw edge, stopping and leaving the last 8″ or so unsewn too. (FIG. D)

5. Beginning in the middle of an edge of your quilt, leave the tail of 8″ and start to pin the binding to the front of quilt, aligning the raw edges. (FIG. E)

6. When you reach a corner, fold the binding back so that the raw edge is in line with the next side of the quilt to be pinned. (FIG. F)

7. Fold the binding back on itself, fold down the resulting tab, and continue to pin the binding to the next side (FIG. G). Repeat for all the corners until you reach the side where you started.

8. Take the two tails and butt them up against each other, making sure they meet neatly, with no slack or excess (FIG. H). Press the creases well.

9. Unfold the two tails and use a disappearing fabric pen to mark the creased line. Without twisting, pin the two tails right sides together and sew along the marked line (FIG. I). Refold the binding and check that it lies smoothly against the quilt.

10. Once you're happy with the fit, trim the sewn seam to ¼″ and press open. Fold the binding in half again, press and pin into position. (FIG. J)

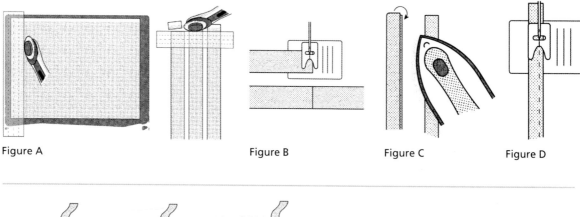

Figure A   Figure B   Figure C   Figure D

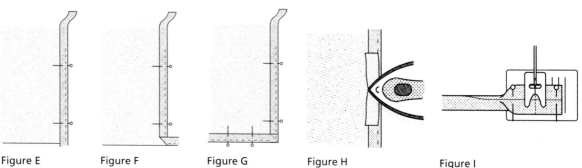

Figure E   Figure F   Figure G   Figure H   Figure I

11. Using a ¼″ seam and beginning in the middle of one edge, sew the binding to the quilt (FIG. K). You may find it helpful to reduce your stitch length a little to give a more secure finish. This is particularly useful if the quilt is likely to see a lot of use.

12. When you get to a corner, stop sewing (with the needle down) ¼″ away from the edge, as indicated by the crease of the mitered corner (FIG. L). You may like to mark the crease so you can see exactly where to stop. Backstitch a few stitches, cut the thread and remove the quilt from the machine.

13. Fold the mitered corner back on itself and begin sewing again along the next edge, one or two stitches in from the edge and backstitching a few stitches at the start (FIG. M). Continue to stitch each edge and corner in this way until you get back to where you began.

14. I recommend stitching around the entire edge of the quilt using a ⅛″ seam allowance securing the raw edges of the binding and the quilt (FIG. N). This gives a more stable edge to fold the binding over and prevents any ridges from forming.

15. Fold the binding over to the back of the quilt and press well. (FIG. O)

16. To finish, I recommend hand sewing the binding using a slipstitch. Start in the middle of an edge and take a stitch every ¼″, catching the lower edge of the binding, not the front of the quilt (FIG. P). At the corners, fold the binding neatly and secure it with a few stitches at the inner corner before continuing along the next side. If you need to re-thread, make a few securing stitches underneath the binding, pass the needle into the quilt sandwich and come out a few inches away. Cut the thread close to the quilt and gently tug the backing.

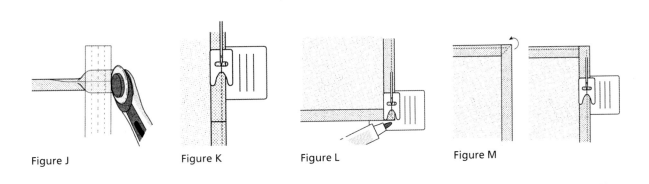

Figure J   Figure K   Figure L   Figure M

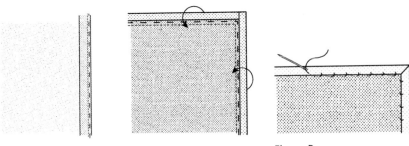

Figure N   Figure O   Figure P

TROUBLESHOOTING

I DELIBERATED over including this chapter for quite some time. The word "troubleshooting" suggests some kind of problem or difficulty that needs to be solved. While we can encounter all sorts of issues when we sew, from broken needles to snapping thread, I want to stress that what may be perceived as an obstacle can, in improv, be an opportunity for creative expression. With liberated sewing, you're not following a pattern or a set of very specific instructions. The techniques we've looked at can and should be interpreted in a way that works for you. There may be times, however, when you feel lost and not sure of the next step to take. It's these "troubles" that I want to shoot down. If you encounter any of these scenarios, find a way to make the experience work for you and don't get too preoccupied by the could-haves and should-haves of sewing.

"I wasn't sure how much fabric to buy and now I've run out."

Because of the nature of improv piecing, it's not always possible to give exact measurements. For this reason, there's always going to be a little bit of guesswork involved. When practicing the techniques, use what you have and don't be afraid to create a scrappier look. With the projects, I've tried to give you the approximate quantities that worked for me. Things like curves and strips can be so varied from quilter to quilter, you may find yourself with some fabric left over or perhaps not quite enough. When you're ready to make a quilt, if you know you want a particular fabric for a particular part, then it's always better to err on the side of caution and purchase a little extra. In instances where that's not possible, embrace the challenge of finding something else that works and see how the quilt evolves.

Don't get too preoccupied by the could-haves and should-haves of sewing.

"My pieces are too small."

What most quilters new to improv struggle with is the lack of information. In one of the first classes I taught, I instructed my students to rummage through their scraps and use scissors to cut a selection of "roughly square" pieces of fabric. The room was quiet as they busied themselves with the task. As I walked around, I could see people reaching for their rulers and rotary cutters. Some called out and asked what size the squares should be. I guess for some quilters these habits are hard to break. The thing with the improv journey is that there's no map. So, after sewing away, creeping ever-closer to the end destination, you may find that some of your units are too small or don't quite fit together in the way you wanted. My suggestion is just to add more fabric! Use the opportunity to add a contrasting strip to one side or sew another unit to fill the gap. What's important is that you don't get too hung up on these little bumps in the road. Use what you have and make the situation work for you.

"My blocks are all different sizes."

This is a good thing! Remember, most of the improv units you'll make aren't designed to fit together. All the math that makes that happen has gone, leaving us with a much more organic and intuitive process. There are variables that are out of our control. Embrace this and use it to your advantage. Don't worry about the finished product in the early stages of liberated sewing. Make decisions freely and spontaneously, creating units of all shapes and sizes. I assure you, despite how much it may not look like it, they'll all come together in the end.

"My seams don't match."

At certain times in my quilting, this is something I actually strive for, putting in as much care to mismatch my seams as others do to make them perfect! This is an area where, if you're not careful, you can become stuck, like a tire in the mud. My advice is to not fixate on it. Perfection isn't the goal here. Press onward with a make-do attitude and show those seams who's boss! Techniques like using stacks and slabs actually benefit from mismatched seams, which all add to a quilt's individuality.

"I don't like what I've sewn."

This isn't unique to improv. Even though we've spent a lot of time choosing the "right" fabrics, there are going to be times when we find that, four blocks in, it's not working. As improvisers, the good thing is we haven't spent hours and hours meticulously cutting pieces and sewing them together with precision. With more traditional blocks, those with defined structure and matched seams, there is little that can be done to remedy a failing fabric pull. We accept the lost time, resign the blocks to a drawer or pass them on, and start again. Liberated sewing affords us a way to work with what we don't like. First, take a time-out and distance yourself from the project. Things can often look different after an hour or even a week. Use the time to create something completely different. Secondly, if you still don't like it when you return to the project, hack into it! Trim it down into small units and piece these together with a fresh fabric. Add something completely surprising and out of your fabric comfort zone to reinvigorate the work and your interest in it.

PART THREE
PROGRESS

In this final part, you'll see how the techniques you've learned can be combined to make a fully realized project. Each quilt is accompanied by an inspirational backstory that tells how I came to the design, fabric notes detailing the colors and prints used, and my initial sketch. This information will give you a further glimpse into my process, and my hope is that after you have attempted one or two of these projects, you'll be inspired to seek out inspiration and design your own quilts. The twelve quilts featured vary in difficulty and can be adapted in many ways. Refer to the How to Use This Book section to individualize the quilts by scaling the units up and down, creating your own color schemes, and experimenting with block layout. I've also given several suggestions for variations that provide further opportunity for personalizing the projects.

Foliage

△▽

Finished size: approximately 45″ × 54″

Quilted by Trudi Wood

Fabric Notes

This quilt works best with hints of prints alongside various solid shades. I pulled three main green colorways; a yellow green, a cool blue green, and a "true" green. Pick three or four solids for each colorway that work well together and throw a few small-scale prints in the mix. Experiment by combining prints that have suggestions of the other greens in them. This will give the whole scheme a feeling of cohesiveness. Look for line prints to draw the eye upward and replicate the minute surface details of the leaves. The thin strips that surround each leaf are the perfect opportunity for a pop of contrast. Don't be afraid to move away from greens here. Mustard and sienna and hot pink would work equally well with the cooler color palette.

Green has always been my favorite color, specifically the rich and varied tones of the plant kingdom. Despite their murderous intentions, I was fascinated by the titular creatures of John Wyndham's The Day of the Triffids, a book which, rather than instill fear, only heightened my interest in plants. Today, my cactus collection, once a few dwarf specimens, now carves out ever-more space in our dining room, like the twisting triffids I was so fascinated by as a child. Our living room houses various potted plants, with leaves of all shapes and sizes: round and flat, tall and spear-like. This quilt is my interpretation of that world. The variegated shards of Sansevieria trifasciata, or snake plant to give it its common name, are perfect for exploring the slab technique and provide a cool and calming color palette. I wanted the quilting to represent the details of the leaves. The horizontal lines on the leaves contrast against the vertical piecing, while the densely quilted background helps to blur the seams of the joined blocks and adds amazing texture. Like the plant itself, you can't help but want to touch this quilt.

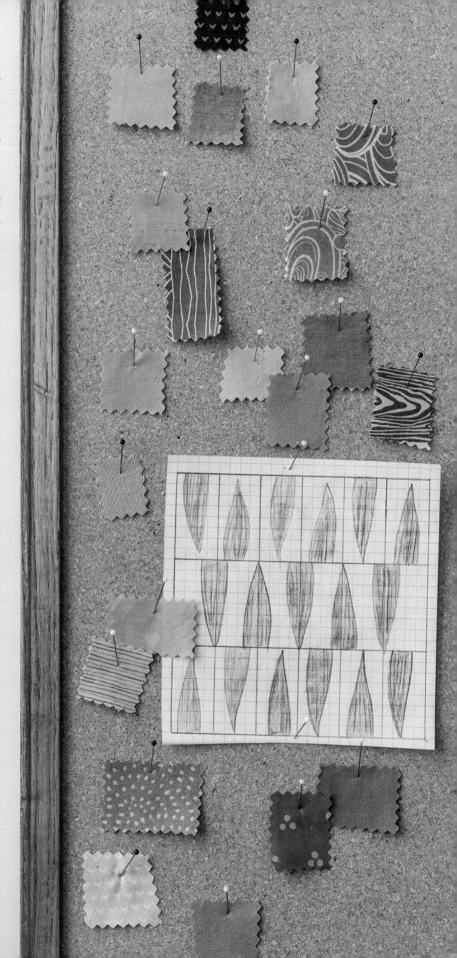

MATERIALS

LEAVES: 5-6 fat eighths in each
of the 3 green colorways

LEAF EDGES: 3-5 fat quarters
in each of the 3 colorways

BACKGROUND FABRIC:
approximately 2½ yards

BATTING: at least 4″ wider
and 4″ longer than your
finished quilt top

BACKING FABRIC: at least 4″
wider and 4″ longer than
your finished quilt top

BINDING FABRIC:
approximately ½ yard

Assembling the Leaves

1. From the leaf fabric, cut a variety of WOF strips between ¾″ and 1¼″ wide. Using the slab technique (see page 44), piece together 17 slabs at least 5″ × 20″ each, being sure to vary the arrangement of the strips. From the leaf edge fabric, cut strips approximately 3″ wide.

2. Position a pieced slab from Step 1 onto your cutting mat and cut a freehand leaf shape from it. The leaf should rise up straight on the sides and curve into a point at the top. Repeat for all 17 slabs.

3. Overlap one side of a leaf on top of a strip of leaf edge fabric, right side up, and cut the curve shape as described in the curve technique (see page 37). Position the leaf edge fabric and the cut leaf right sides together and sew the curve. Press the seam towards the outer edge and trim to approximately ½″, following the line of the curve.

4. Repeat Step 3 for the other side of the leaf.

5. Repeat Steps 3-4 to create a total of 17 leaf blocks.

6. Cut 2 approximately 4″ × 20″ rectangles from the background fabric. Using the curve technique, attach a background rectangle to both sides of a leaf unit from Step 5. Cut the curve, then place right sides together leaving some background fabric extending past both ends of the leaf and sew. Press well. Repeat for a total of 15 leaf units.

7. The last two blocks are constructed in the same way, only with wider pieces of background fabric on one side. These will be the ends of the middle row, so add these extra-wide rectangles to the left side of one leaf and to the right side of the other.

Completing the Quilt Top

1. Arrange the leaf units into 3 rows: 6 leaves in the top and bottom rows and 5 leaves in the middle. Stagger their placement so that the tips of the leaves in the middle row and bottom row fall between the leaves of the previous row.

2. Once you're happy with the arrangement, trim the excess fabric away from either end of the middle row to approximately 11¾″ × 18½″ and all the other blocks to approximately 8″ × 18½″.

3. Sew the blocks into rows, pressing the seams of the different rows in alternate directions to allow the seams to interlock. Sew the rows together and press to complete the quilt top.

Finishing

1. Baste the quilt top using your preferred method, making sure all three layers are nice and smooth. Quilt as desired.

2. Cut the binding fabric into 2″ strips and sew together, end-to-end. Press the seams open. Press the binding in half along the width, wrong sides together, and use to finish the quilt (see page 62 for my binding method).

Get Inspired

When joining the strips, don't worry about the distortion that can happen when pressing longer slabs of strips — in fact, aim for this and use the bend as inspiration when cutting the shape of your leaf. It's quicker and easier to press the slab as a whole piece rather than after each addition.

Variations

▷ Some varieties of snake plants have short, wider leaves. Experiment with the shapes you cut from the slabs and combine tall and squat units to add variety to the quilt.

▷ To emphasize the shorter leaf shapes, turn the slabs 90 degrees before cutting the leaf so that the strips are horizontal.

▷ Use a reduced color palette or only solids to represent a minimalist interpretation of the plant.

▷ Combine with different shaped leaves, pieced together using the jigsaw method (see page 54), to create a dense display of improv foliage.

Quilting Notes

Trudi has done such an amazing job taking my inspiration and transferring it to the quilting. The leaves have been quilted with gentle hooks that mimic the surface patterns. For the background, I wanted something that would disguise the seam lines. Dense echoing does this and adds movement to the negative space.

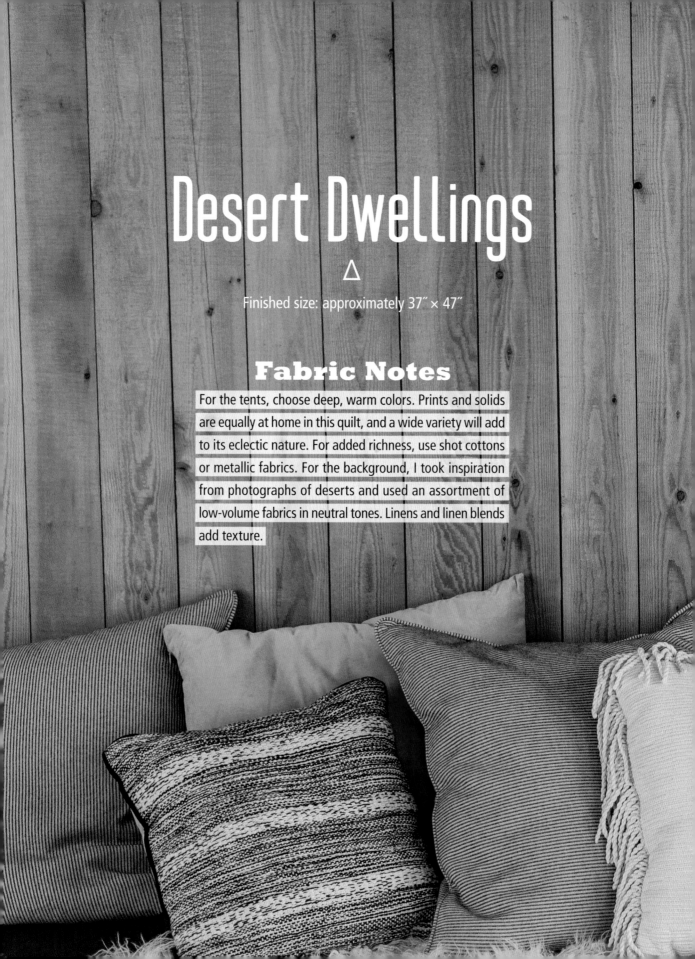

Desert Dwellings

△

Finished size: approximately 37" × 47"

Fabric Notes

For the tents, choose deep, warm colors. Prints and solids are equally at home in this quilt, and a wide variety will add to its eclectic nature. For added richness, use shot cottons or metallic fabrics. For the background, I took inspiration from photographs of deserts and used an assortment of low-volume fabrics in neutral tones. Linens and linen blends add texture.

I'll always be drawn to rich jewel tones. One place that holds a high spot on my list of holiday destinations is Marrakech, Morocco. The colorful sights, sounds, and smells of the souks are so inspiring. I imagine myself getting lost for hours in the meandering alleys and backstreets, buying silks and spices to take home to cook and create with. The inspiration for this quilt comes from both the saturated colors of the marketplace and the nomadic tents found on the desert outskirts, lit from within by bright candlelight. This quilt is a simple but effective way of using triangle units and can be adapted to suit any size or layout.

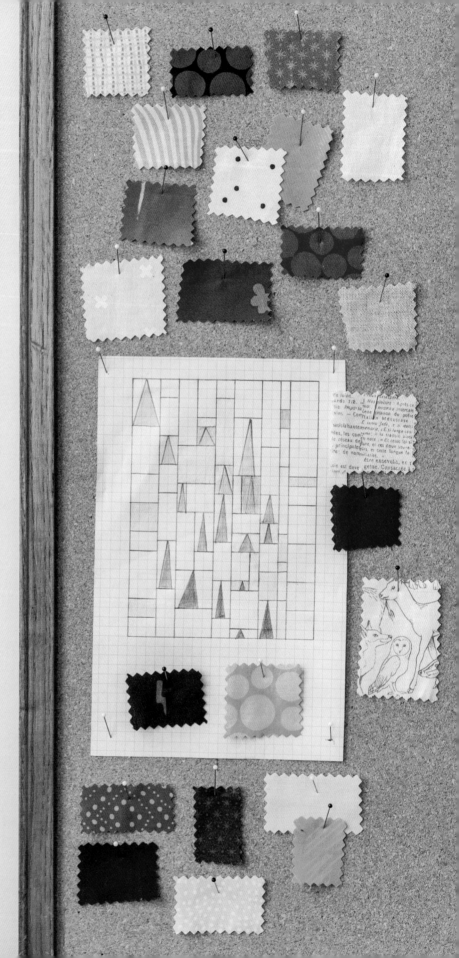

MATERIALS

TENTS: scraps of colored fabrics

BACKGROUND: large
scraps of neutral fabric

BATTING: at least 4″ wider
and 4″ longer than your
finished quilt top

BACKING FABRIC: at least 4″
wider and 4″ longer than
your finished quilt top

BINDING FABRIC:
approximately ½ yard

Piecing the Triangles

1. Use the triangle technique (see page 50) to make triangle units. You can make the quilt as busy as you like. If creating a lot of units, it is quicker to chain piece all the right background pieces first, clip and press, then chain piece the left background pieces. Be sure to keep your background pieces in order, as well as the triangle pieces when you clip and press them.

Completing the Quilt Top

1. Arrange the triangle units into a pleasing composition. You may prefer to bring some of the triangles units up to size first by adding background fabric to any number of sides.

2. Once you're happy with the layout, sew them together using the jigsaw method (see page 54).

Finishing

1. Baste the quilt top using your preferred method, making sure all three layers are nice and smooth. Quilt as desired.

2. Cut the binding fabric into 2″ strips and sew together, end-to-end. Press the seams open. Press the binding in half along the width, wrong sides together, and use to finish the quilt (see page 62 for my binding method).

Get Inspired

Try not to think about the composition of the quilt until you have a good number of triangles to work with. This way, when you come to arrange the units, you can see if you're lacking triangles in a particular print or size. Remember, you can always save any extra to piece into the backing or use them in your next quilt.

Variations

▷ Rather than arranging the triangle units in color order, piece them randomly into the quilt top for a scrappier look.

▷ Use darker fabrics for the background to suggest a desert at night. Piece snippets of white fabric into these dark fabrics to give the look of stars in the night sky.

▷ Make a wider range of triangle sizes and arrange the units from small to large. You could radiate out from the center of the quilt or work from edge-to-edge.

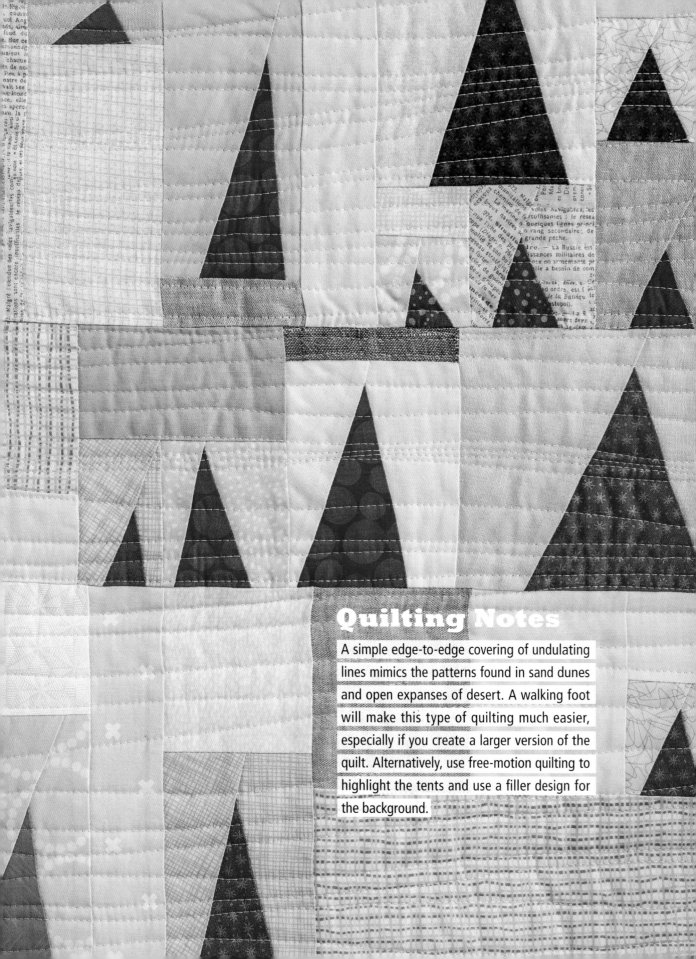

Quilting Notes

A simple edge-to-edge covering of undulating lines mimics the patterns found in sand dunes and open expanses of desert. A walking foot will make this type of quilting much easier, especially if you create a larger version of the quilt. Alternatively, use free-motion quilting to highlight the tents and use a filler design for the background.

How to Age a Tree

△▽△

Finished size: approximately 68″ × 68″

Quilted by Trudi Wood

Fabric Notes

I wanted my tree to have a range of wood colors, from rust reds to the darkest browns. To represent the tree's spring growth, the fabric pull was much more limited. I alternated between three to four different light fabrics to tie the successive rings together. Be sure to include pops of contrasting fabrics to show your tree's various life moments. Blue-green works well against the red-oranges, but you can add snippets of whatever you like. Since most of the rings end up quite narrow, small-scale prints work well as do solids, especially several tones of one shade. Look for prints with organic lines or crosshatching on them to emphasize the nature of the wood. Shot cottons work beautifully to add a depth and richness to this quilt.

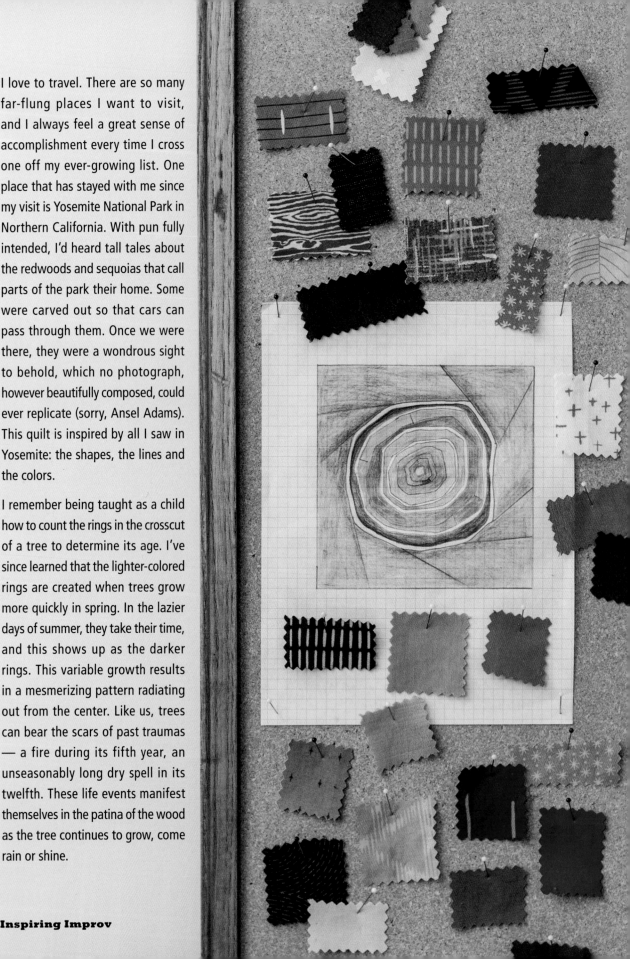

I love to travel. There are so many far-flung places I want to visit, and I always feel a great sense of accomplishment every time I cross one off my ever-growing list. One place that has stayed with me since my visit is Yosemite National Park in Northern California. With pun fully intended, I'd heard tall tales about the redwoods and sequoias that call parts of the park their home. Some were carved out so that cars can pass through them. Once we were there, they were a wondrous sight to behold, which no photograph, however beautifully composed, could ever replicate (sorry, Ansel Adams). This quilt is inspired by all I saw in Yosemite: the shapes, the lines and the colors.

I remember being taught as a child how to count the rings in the crosscut of a tree to determine its age. I've since learned that the lighter-colored rings are created when trees grow more quickly in spring. In the lazier days of summer, they take their time, and this shows up as the darker rings. This variable growth results in a mesmerizing pattern radiating out from the center. Like us, trees can bear the scars of past traumas — a fire during its fifth year, an unseasonably long dry spell in its twelfth. These life events manifest themselves in the patina of the wood as the tree continues to grow, come rain or shine.

DARKER RINGS: 26-30 fabrics,
¼ yard cuts work best

LIGHTER RINGS: 4-6 fabrics,
½ yard of each

CONTRASTING FABRICS: scrap
strips or cut from yardage

BACKGROUND FABRIC:
approximately 2-3 yards
(needed to make the tree "float")

BATTING: at least 4″ wider
and 4″ longer than your
finished quilt top

BACKING FABRIC: at least 4″
wider and 4″ longer than
your finished quilt top

BINDING FABRIC:
approximately ½ yard

Piecing the Trunk

1. Begin by arranging the darker fabrics in the order they are to appear. I transitioned from creams to browns, oranges, reds, dark browns and finally blacks. Take a snippet of each fabric and add it to a design wall or inspiration board for easy reference while piecing. From one light fabric, cut an approximate 5″ square and draw a circle on it as described in the ring technique (see page 42). This will be the center of the tree.

2. From the remaining darker fabrics, cut WOF strips varying from ¾″ to 2½″. Rings closer to the center will obviously need less fabric than those towards the outer edge. If you are sure of the width of each ring, I recommend cutting all the strips first. If you would like to work a bit more improvisationally, cut each fabric when you are ready to sew it into the quilt top.

3. Trim a strip of the first darker fabric and sew the first piece of the ring. Continue to add pieces of this fabric until the ring is complete.

4. Continue in this way, alternating between light and dark fabrics, until you reach a diameter you're happy with. My tree trunk finished at approximately 68″. The freedom to cut your rings to any size will result in your quilt having more or fewer rings than my version. Every few rings, add some pieces in a contrasting fabric to represent events in the tree's past. This can be a single piece or several pieces in the ring. A snippet can also be pieced into one of strips and then attached. To mimic the natural growth of trees, vary the width of each complete ring and re-cut some of the angles create an irregular shape.

Completing the Quilt Top

At this stage, the quilt can be squared up as it is, so that the rings of the tree extend beyond the edges of the quilt. Or, to make the crosscut tree "float" in a diptych, larger pieces need to be added to the final ring to act as a background. The background strips are cut much wider than the rings but are attached in the same way. I recommend using string or masking tape to mark out the desired perimeter of the quilt on a wall or similar large surface to have an idea of the area needed to be filled with background fabric. Return the quilt top to the perimeter guide after each addition to check the coverage.

Finishing

1. Baste the quilt top using your preferred method, making sure all three layers are nice and smooth. Quilt as desired.

2. Cut the binding fabric into 2″ strips and sew together, end-to-end. Press the seams open. Press the binding in half along the width, wrong sides together, and use to finish the quilt (see page 62 for my binding method).

Get Inspired

Owing to the large number of cuts and the resulting bias edges, there is a chance of some distortion and fullness when using the ring technique. When I made the leek block, which is tiny in comparison to this quilt, the fullness was easily minimized by a vigorous press before being quilted out entirely. My How to Age a Tree quilt provided an entirely different challenge, one which at the same time tested my ability as a quilt maker and solidified my love for improv. You can read more about how I navigated this particularly bad "snowstorm of sewing" in the Afterword, A Quilt of Two Halves.

Variations

▷ Use a limited fabric pull, with one for the spring rings and another for the summer.

▷ Reverse the order so that the darker fabrics are at the center and get progressively lighter as the tree grows.

▷ Make several smaller ring units, then cut each in half and sew to another for a scrappier look.

Quilting Notes

From my earliest sketches, I knew that the only option for the tree portion of this quilt would be wood grain. The quilting of the background took a little more thought. After considering pebbling and swirls, I ultimately decided upon an echoing of the trunk shape to emphasize the rings. Again, Trudi has elevated the piecing and made the quilt sing.

The Night Garden

△

Finished size: approximately 60″ × 60″

Fabric Notes

The quilt is made up of five types of blocks designed to give the effect of a densely planted garden. As you move up the quilt, the amount of green lessens, giving way to pinks, purples, and finally the dark indigos of the sky. For the lower part of the quilt, cool blue-green fabrics in various tones work best. For the flowers, violets, blue-violets, and hot pinks add a brightness without making the color scheme too warm. Remember, this is the Night Garden after all. The dark blues of the sky portion are dotted with whites and silvery grays, like stars in the night sky. You'll only need snippets of these, so use what you have.

Don't be afraid to choose bold and bright fabrics for this quilt: florals, geometrics, lines, and focal prints. An eclectic looks best, so use a large variety. Add in some coordinating solids to give the eye a resting place among the busier prints. The snippets of fabric in some of the strips are a great place to add a fussy-cut focal print. Look for fabrics with bold floral designs, insects, and birds to add a sense of whimsy to the quilt.

This quilt is a re-imagining of one I made in the autumn of 2014. Entitled Blooming Borders, it was my interpretation of a garden in full flower and was a way of bringing some color to an otherwise gray October. This was the quilt that introduced me to the subtle art of the freehand curve and is a personal favorite of mine. I wanted to explore a similar theme with this version, but with a drastically different color palette. For this night-time feel, I took inspiration from the paintings of the French naïve painter Henri Rousseau, more specifically, his lush and exotic depictions of jungles. The Dream is the largest of the jungle paintings, full of foliage, flowers, and animals. A reclining nude reaches towards a snake charmer, partly hidden by the dim light of the full moon. It was this cool dusk I wanted to capture: the idea of moonlight glinting over leaves and flower heads, highlighting their jewel-like tones.

Piecing the Blocks

1. Cut each of the long quarters into (3) 3″ × WOF strips. Cut each strip into (3) 3″ × 13½″ pieces, saving the offcuts.

2. Using the curve technique (see page 37), join strips to make 25 blocks, each a little larger than 12½″ square. Refer to the table below to create 5 blocks of each of the 5 types.

A Blocks	blue-green strips with 2-3 purple-pink scraps in 2 or 3 of the blocks
B Blocks	blue-green strips with 6-8 purple-pink scraps in each block
C Blocks	blue-green and purple-pink strips with 6-8 green and purple-pink scraps in each block
D Blocks	purple-pink strips with purple-pink scraps and 2-3 blue scraps in 2 or 3 of the blocks
E Blocks	purple-pink and blue strips with 1-2 purple-pink scraps and 4-6 white scraps in each block

3. Press each block well before trimming to 12½″ square.

Completing the Quilt Top

1. Arrange each type of block into a row. Then arrange the rows, with the A blocks as the bottom row, the B blocks the row above it, C, then D and finally the E blocks as the top row.

2. When you are happy with the arrangement, sew the blocks together into rows, pressing the seams of the different rows in alternate directions to allow the seams to interlock. Sew the rows together and press to complete the quilt top.

BLUE-GREEN FABRIC: 10-12¼ yards

PURPLE AND HOT PINK FABRICS: 10-12 ¼ yards

DARK BLUE FABRIC: 4-6¼ yards

Scraps of WHITE AND GRAY FABRIC

BATTING: at least 4″ wider and 4″ longer than your finished quilt top

BACKING FABRIC: at least 4″ wider and 4″ longer than your finished quilt top

BINDING FABRIC: approximately ½ yard

Finishing

1. Baste the quilt top using your preferred method, making sure all three layers are nice and smooth. Quilt as desired.

2. Cut the binding fabric into 2″ strips and sew together, end-to-end. Press the seams open. Press the binding in half along the width, wrong sides together, and use to finish the quilt (see page 62 for my binding method).

Get Inspired

The number of strips you need for each block will depend on how wavy you cut your curves. I found I needed 8-10 strips to make each block large enough to be trimmed down to 12½″ square. It may be helpful to lay out your strips in groups before you begin sewing. Use the photographs of the finished quilt as a guide for placing your strips and scraps. In the E blocks, the first few strips should be purple before transitioning to blue. As you insert more scraps into the strips and square up the blocks, you can use the offcuts as inserts for other blocks.

Variations

▷ Use a color pull of bright greens coupled with yellows, oranges, and softer pinks for the floral section to create a garden in the height of summer. Use sky blues and bright whites for the sky section.

▷ Omit the sky section and use the top row to continue the garden to the edge of the quilt.

▷ Rather than trim the blocks to a universal size, make lots of different size units of strips and piece them together using the jigsaw method (see page 54). This will give you a real freedom with the layout and add to the organic look of the quilt.

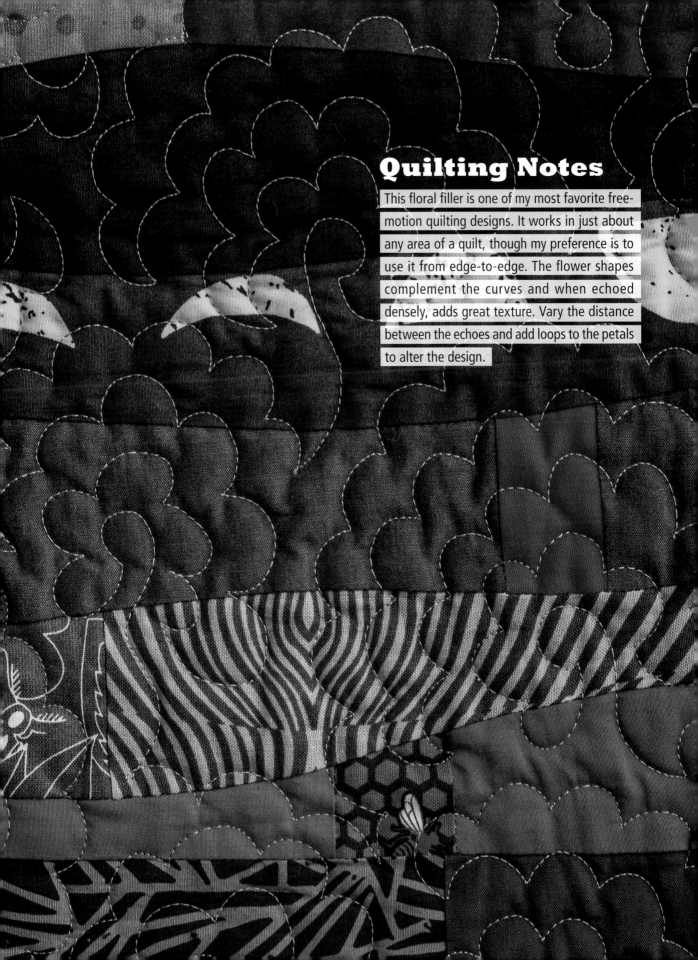

Quilting Notes

This floral filler is one of my most favorite free-motion quilting designs. It works in just about any area of a quilt, though my preference is to use it from edge-to-edge. The flower shapes complement the curves and when echoed densely, adds great texture. Vary the distance between the echoes and add loops to the petals to alter the design.

Tally

△▽

Finished size: approximately 56″ × 58″

Fabric Notes

Variety is key. Yes, the color palette may be limited, but by using a large number of background fabrics you'll better convey that many-pieces-of-paper feel. Look for neutrals in whites, creams, and taupe. Avoid busy prints for this quilt. You don't want anything to distract from the tallies. With the exception of some small pieces of tone-on-tone crosshatch fabric, my quilt is made entirely of solids. Add interest by using linen and linen blends alongside cottons. For the tallies, I used the classic ball-point pen colors of blue, black, and red, with some gray to suggest pencil marks. I stuck to saturated solids for these too, so that they really stand out from the background.

A tally, or tally stick, was an ancient means of recording numbers and quantities. Marco Polo mentions their use in 13th century China in his recounting tales of his travels, and centuries later they are still used to aid the memory of anyone who needs to keep count. Today, they are more recognizable as the marks we make on paper, usually clustered in groups of five for quick arithmetic. We use them to keep score in games, to count knitted rows, and, in the case of many incarcerated characters of Hollywood's golden age, to count down the long days until their release! I remember being taught as a child the way to make the marks. First, place the fence posts I, II, III, and IIII, then, in a final fifth stroke, hitch the gate across the posts.

The inspiration for this quilt only came once I'd started working on some of the others for this book. I had notes everywhere — bits of paper in files and folders, pinned to notice boards and stuck to walls — all different sizes and covered with a chicken scratch of many colors. An organized person would have used a notebook so that everything was together. I clearly preferred to grab the nearest pen and scribble away on scraps. This quilt is my interpretation of those moments.

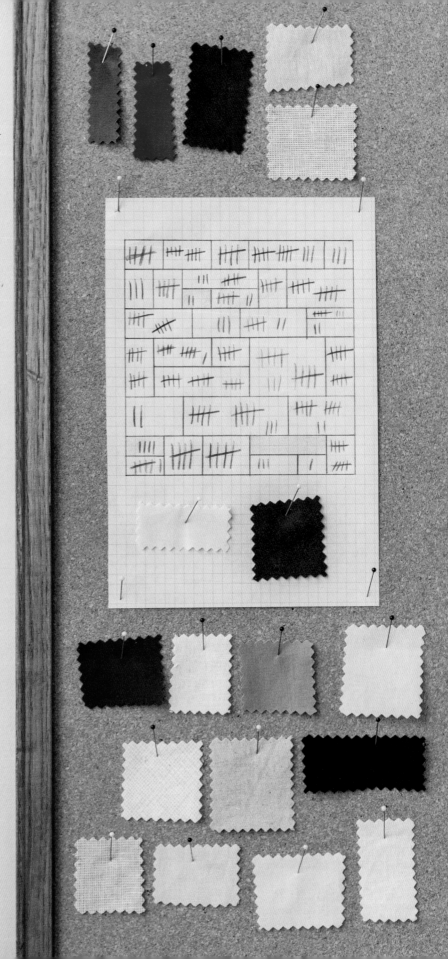

Piecing the Tally Units

1. Cut each long quarter of tally fabric into a variety of WOF strips, from ¾″ to 1½″ wide. Cut each of the strips in half along the length. Don't worry about being too accurate, as these measurements are only a guide.

2. Cut each of the half-yard background fabrics into 7″ × WOF strips. Cut each of the strips in half along the length.

3. Take a background strip and, using the insert technique (see page 39), make up to 4 cuts along the whole width. Be sure to vary the distance between them. Sew a colored tally strip into each cut and press the seams well.

4. Continue to make slabs in this way, inserting 1, 2, 3, or 4 tally strips into the background strips.

5. Subcut the slabs into different sized units to add variation to the quilt.

6. Choose a unit with 4 tally strips and make another cut across the inserted strips. Piece a strip into this cut to complete the tally of five. Make more five-tally units in the same way.

Completing the Quilt Top

1. Arrange the units, using the photograph of the finished quilt on the next page as a reference. Randomly choose some units to add additional background fabric to one or more sides. This part will be dictated by the variety of the units, so take time to find an arrangement that works. Fill any gaps with extra background fabric as needed.

2. Once you're happy with the arrangement, use the jigsaw method (see page 54) to complete the quilt top.

Finishing

1. Baste the quilt top using your preferred method, making sure all three layers are nice and smooth. Quilt as desired.

2. Cut the binding fabric into 2″ strips and sew together, end-to-end. Press the seams open. Press the binding in half along the width, with the wrong sides together and use to finish the quilt (see page 62 for my binding method).

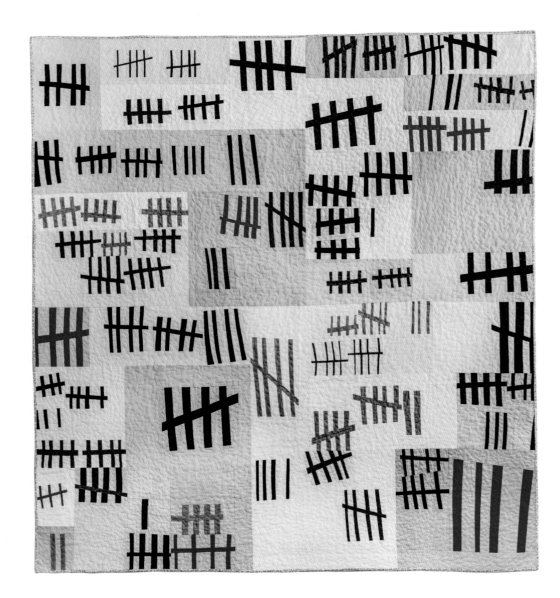

Get Inspired

Don't worry about trimming the inserts to the exact length needed. Save time by roughly cutting to size and deal with any overhang when the unit is straightened up.

Variations

▷ Use black and dark gray fabrics for the background and white or pastel-colored solids for the inserts to give the quilt a chalkboard look.

▷ Make units and piece them into the quilt top in numerical order. Start in the top left corner and move down the length of the quilt, increasing the tally as you go.

▷ Create a minimal look by using the same fabric for the background and fewer tally units. Or, make three or four larger units and offset them within the composition of the quilt.

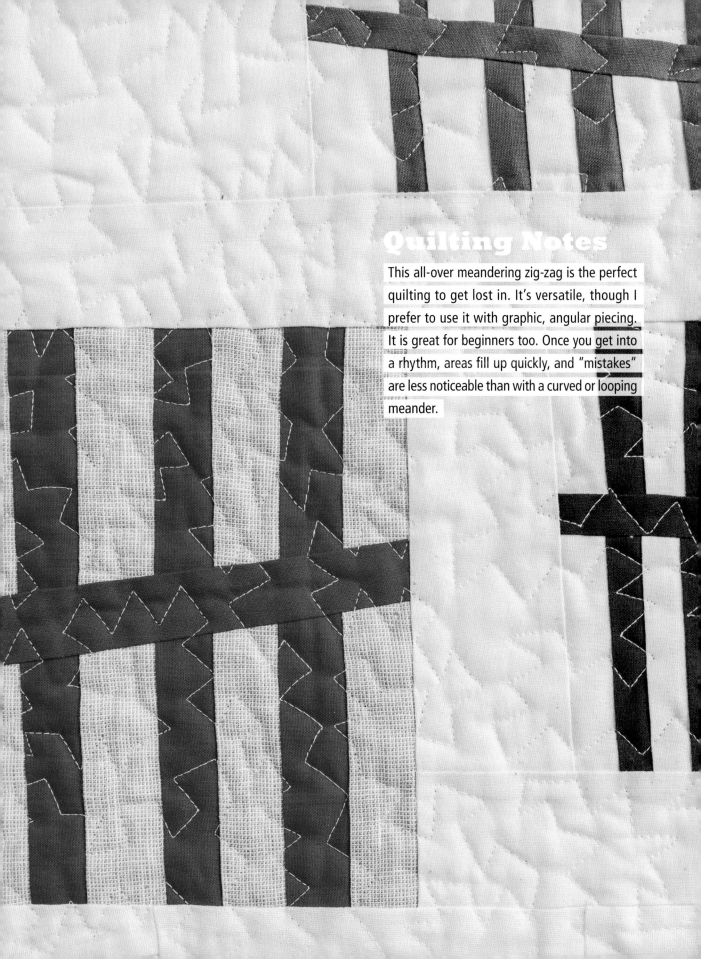

Quilting Notes

This all-over meandering zig-zag is the perfect quilting to get lost in. It's versatile, though I prefer to use it with graphic, angular piecing. It is great for beginners too. Once you get into a rhythm, areas fill up quickly, and "mistakes" are less noticeable than with a curved or looping meander.

Shoal

△▽

Finished size: approximately 32″ × 35″

Fabric Notes

My color palette was inspired by silvery sardines swimming in the deep ocean, where shallower waters give way to plunging depths that little or no sunlight penetrates. Whether scientifically accurate or not, the snippets of white and gray against the dark, saturated background, make for a striking quilt. Look for a range of blues, avoiding anything too bright. Solids work well alongside tone-on-tone prints. Try to keep these within the same color family. Snippets of sea green add depth to the background. For the fish, use whites and soft grays, with the odd darker print mixed in among the shoal. Metallic fabrics and shot cottons work well to suggest what little light there is glinting off scales.

As you've probably realized by now, I take a lot of inspiration from the natural world. As a child, I was fascinated by wildlife and was an avid watcher of anything on TV narrated by Sir David Attenborough. I remember giving myself projects to complete over the summer holidays. I'd research an animal, say sharks or orangutans, and compile my finding in a folder full of facts. Images would fill the pages, either clipped from magazines or crudely drawn by my own hand. Drawing is something I've never been that good at but have always wanted to be. Among many other things, my grandmother taught me the rudimentary shapes of many creatures, which I'd practice over and over: cats, snakes, fish. It was that naïve interpretation that inspired this quilt. This simplistic version of a shoal of fish reminds me of my childhood and the simple line drawings that occupied me for hours.

MATERIALS

FISH: an assortment of large white and gray scraps, totaling approximately ½ yard

BACKGROUND: an assortment of large dark blue scraps, totaling approximately 1 yard

Small scraps of **GREEN-BLUE FABRIC**

BATTING: at least 4″ wider and 4″ longer than your finished quilt top

BACKING FABRIC: at least 4″ wider and 4″ longer than your finished quilt top

BINDING FABRIC: approximately ¼ yard

Piecing the Fish Units

1. Make a fish tail using the triangle technique (see page 50) from a square of white or gray fabric and two larger blue scraps for the background.

2. Next, make a curved fish body. Using the curve technique (see page 37), place a piece of fish fabric and background fabric on the cutting mat, overlapping the long edge. Cut the first curve and sew. Repeat for the other side, making sure to allow the fabric to extend past the top and bottom of the body by at least ¼″.

3. Use a ruler and rotary cutter to straighten the apex edge of the triangle fish tail unit, making sure to leave a ¼″ seam allowance if the whole triangle will be the tail. Repeat for the body piece, straightening the edge that will be sewn to the tail unit. I recommend placing the tail unit next to the body before cutting, to evaluate how it will look when pieced together. Remember to add a ¼″ seam allowance to the body unit too.

4. Repeat until there are enough tail and body units to fill the finished size the project requires. For my quilt, I made 28 of each, giving me 28 finished fish, varying from 4″ to 12″. The finished size of your fish is determined by the size of the triangle and curved units. Be sure to make a variety of sizes.

5. Join a tail and body unit of the same fabric together, taking care to align them properly. Repeat with the remaining tails and bodies.

Completing the Quilt Top

1. Arrange the pieced fish units using the photographs of the finished quilt on the next page as a guide. Try to create movement within the quilt by leaving space between some fish and placing others close together. Fill any gaps with extra background fabric and scraps of blue-green fabric.

2. Once you're happy with the arrangement, use the jigsaw method (see page 54) to complete the quilt top.

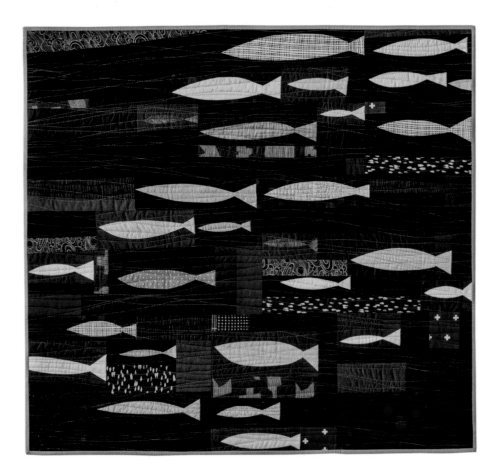

Finishing

1. Baste the quilt top using your preferred method, making sure all three layers are nice and smooth. Quilt as desired.

2. Cut the binding fabric into 2″ strips and sew together, end-to-end. Press the seams open. Press the binding in half along the width, wrong sides together, and use to finish the quilt (see page 62 for my binding method).

Get Inspired

To add variation to your shoal, cut some of the tail unit edges farther into the triangle so that the point is lost. Normally, quilters mourn the loss of a point, but here it works to add further interest and makes each fish in the shoal distinctly different.

Variations

▷ Use a bright fabric pull to create a Caribbean look. Use an eclectic mix of spotty, striped, and densely printed fabrics to add lots of variety and mimic the patterns of tropical fish.

▷ Make curved units in green fabrics and join them in columns. Piece them vertically into the quilt around the fish units to suggest kelp and seaweed.

▷ Piece the units together using curved seams. To make this easier, add extra background fabric around the fish units to give you the space needed to cut the curves.

Quilting Notes

As in Desert Dwellings, this quilt is
perfectly suited to an edge-to-edge- not-
quite-straight-line quilting treatment. Use
it to suggest waves and the movement of
water. For variation, add some pebbling
behind the fish to mimic bubbles as they
swim away.

Liberated Log Cabin

Finished size: approximately 54″ × 54″

Fabric Notes

When it comes to log cabins, anything goes: solids, prints or a mash-up of the two. For this quilt, I began by choosing several prints that worked together well. Don't be worried about using larger prints for this project. Even though they'll eventually be trimmed down to narrow logs, the secondary patterns that emerge from such cutting can add a whole new look to the finished quilt. Once I was happy with my prints, I rummaged the solids for both coordinating and contrasting colors. I used regular cotton, shot cotton, and even a lightweight denim to add both visual and tactile interest. To tie the whole piece together, use a coordinating filler fabric that works with your chosen palette and adds small areas of restful negative space. I find that log cabins work best with a harmonious color scheme punctuated by several contrasting colors for interest. Blind pulling your strips from a bag really adds to the spontaneity of this quilt.

Of all the quilts in this book, this is most inspired by traditionalism. The ubiquitous appearance of the pattern is what first drew me to quilt making. I'd seen so many log cabin quilts draped over beds or hung on the walls of colonial farmhouses. I had read about how the center square, traditionally cut from red fabric, represented the hearth of the fire, the keystone of family life. I was intrigued by the construction and couldn't wait to attempt the pattern for myself.

I used the stack technique (see page 46) to create starter centers, then blind pulled from a bag of strips to bring the blocks up to size. Using this method, the blocks come together quickly so that a long cutting list of a traditionally pieced block is avoided. I threw in some half-square triangle centers to some of the log cabins to add a different shape. There really is no right or wrong way to piece the log cabins. You can make as many blocks as you want and then fill in the rest of the quilt with background fabric.

Variety is the key. For some of your blocks, sew to each side in a clockwise or counter-clockwise direction. For others, skip a side or add several strips to one side. Add to opposite sides for a "courthouse steps" effect or to two sides for a bento-box-style log cabin.

MATERIALS

STARTER UNITS: large selection of 4″ to 6″ squares

OUTER LOGS: large selection of WOF strips of varying widths

BACKGROUND: extra yardage of coordinating fabric, approximately ½ yard

BATTING: at least 4″ wider and 4″ longer than your finished quilt top

BACKING FABRIC: at least 4″ wider and 4″ longer than your finished quilt top

BINDING FABRIC: approximately ⅜ yard

If you want to add some "wonk" to your logs, trim one side at a slight angle before attaching a strip to that side. Do this once, a dozen times or not at all. Remember, variation is the key!

Piecing the Log Cabins

1. Using the log cabin method found in the stacks technique (see page 46), make a variety of blocks. Consider featuring an improv half-square triangle in the center, using the triangle technique (see page 53). It may be necessary to trim the sides slightly so that they match the logs.

2. Place the strips for the outer logs into a bag. Draw one blindly and position it right side up. Place a starter unit right sides together, along the long edge of the strip. Sew the unit in place, sew a few stitches along, then place and sew another unit to the strip. Add a few units in this way before cutting the strip and blindly choosing another strip from the bag. Sew more starter units to this strip and continue in this way until all your starter units are sewn to a variety of strips.

3. Separate each starter unit pair along the strip and press the seam. I recommend pressing towards the center square each time a log is added.

4. Continue to sew successive strips to the starter units. Be sure to use a variety of different width strips in each block. Make some of the blocks "full" log cabins — that is, keep adding strips until the block is the desired size (or slightly bigger so they can be trimmed if needed). For other blocks, make smaller log cabins and bring the block to size using the background fabric, adding to some or all of the sides.

5. Once there are enough blocks for the desired size of quilt you want to make, press well and trim them to size. In my version, I made 36 blocks, each large enough so that it could be trimmed to 9½″ square, giving me a finished quilt size of approximately 54″ square.

Completing the Quilt Top

1. Take the time to play with the block arrangement. The coordinating background fabric in each block works to create blank areas when placed side by side. This negative space will help the busy piecing breathe and give the eye somewhere to rest.

2. Once you're happy with the arrangement, sew the blocks together into rows. Press the seams of the different rows in alternate directions to allow them to interlock. Sew the rows together and press to complete the quilt top.

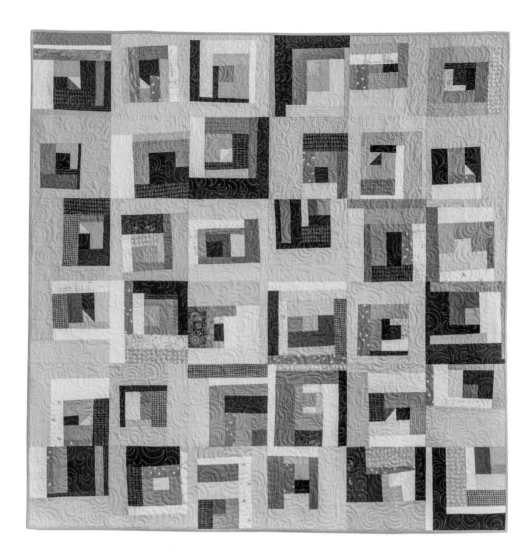

Finishing

See page 74 for Finishing instructions.

Get Inspired

Due to the variation in the width of the logs and the added wonky cutting, this method of making log cabin blocks may result in your center square no longer being centered — and that's okay!

Variations

▷ Make the strips the same width for a more structured look. Use the stack technique (see page 46) to make larger starting units. Cut these in half or into quarters before mixing them up and sewing back together.

▷ Make your quilt top one large log cabin. Once the WOF strips are no longer big enough, join two together to continue adding logs.

Quilting Notes

How you quilt your quilts is a great opportunity to add contrast. We often talk about contrast in the context of choosing fabrics for our quilts. You can use the quilting to add curves and loops to straight blocks, or angular lines to curved piecing. With curved quilting, experiment with both gentle and sharp curves. On this quilt, the quilting idea stemmed from the colors and prints: tones of honey and caramel with glimpses of wasps. All I could think about was a bumbling bear gate-crashing a picnic. The quilting represents his claws, swiping at the sweet fare.

Drunken Tiles

△

Finished size: approximately 48″ × 54″

Fabric Notes

I'm going to tell you a secret. All-solid quilts scare me. This probably has something to do with my chaotic brain and magpie-like attraction to pattern. We all know the good that can come from stepping out of your comfort zone; I've been encouraging you nonstop to do it throughout this book. For this quilt, I wanted to challenge myself to sew without prints. I asked my good friend Nydia to choose a color pull for one of the projects in this book, and this is the result. Asking someone whose eye for color is different from yours is a great way to bring something unexpected to your quilt making and to force you to step away from your usual choices. The resulting pull is soft with punches of navy, though you can see that one print sneakily found its way in! Have fun experimenting when you make this quilt, mixing contrasting and complementary colors. I often like to have a harmonious selection with one or two rebellious colors thrown into the mix. Use the triangular pieces to add extra interest to as much of the quilt top as you like.

The original version of this quilt holds a special place in my heart. It was my first published pattern and the first time I'd made a quilt that others may possibly attempt to make themselves. I was inspired by an entranceway I'd seen, beautifully tiled in a geometric pattern. Over the years, some misfortune had caused a section to crack, and whoever attempted the repair, however valiant the effort, had failed to align the pieces of the pattern, resulting in a mismatch of grout lines. It was as if the tiles were drunk, stumbling about the place and bumping into their neighbors. Inspiration struck and my Drunken Tiles quilt was born. Since then, I've made many versions of this quilt. The stack technique provides ample opportunities for creative expression and is the perfect introduction to improv sewing. The resulting units have an air of the traditional about them while still being uniquely liberated. You could make this quilt ten times over and each one would be so different.

FAT QUARTERS: 12-14

CONTRASTING FABRIC: Small
scraps cut into triangles

BATTING: at least 4″ wider
and 4″ longer than your
finished quilt top

BACKING FABRIC: at least 4″
wider and 4″ longer than
your finished quilt top

BINDING FABRIC:
approximately ½ yard

Piecing the Blocks

1. From the fat quarters, cut 48 approximately 7½″ × 10 ½″ rectangles. In my version, I used ochre and brown fabrics for the "centers" of the tiles. If you have a particular mix of colors you'd like to use for the centers, you will need 12 rectangles of these fabrics and 36 of your other fabrics. Alternatively, you can use a random assortment of fabrics and have no defined "center." From the smaller scraps, cut squares and then halve them to give 2 triangles. There is no specific quantity needed for this quilt, so use what you have and don't be afraid to mix fabrics.

2. Arrange the rectangles into 12 stacks of 4. If you are using a particular fabric or color as the center of the blocks, make sure each stack has this fabric/color in it once.

3. Using the stack technique (see page 46), cut and sew each stack until you have 48 units.

4. Arrange the units into a 6 × 8 grid, using the photograph on the next page as a guide. There is no right or wrong way to arrange the units. You can group like-fabrics together to create secondary shapes or distribute them throughout the quilt top for a more random look.

5. Use the triangles of contrasting fabric throughout to create movement in specific areas or place them entirely at random. I recommend laying the triangles on top of the units to check the placement before making cuts. Step back often to check your progress. Once you are ready to sew, cut the corner of the corresponding unit, sew the triangle to the cut edge, and press. Continue adding triangles as desired. These little snippets of interest will really come to life once the blocks are pieced together. At this stage, it's a good idea to label your blocks or take a photograph of them as a reminder of your chosen layout.

6. Press the blocks well and trim each to 6½″ × 9½″.

Completing the Quilt Top

Sew the blocks together into rows, pressing the seams of the different rows in alternate directions to allowing them to interlock. Sew the rows together and press to complete the quilt top.

Finishing

1. Baste the quilt top using your preferred method, making sure all three layers are nice and smooth. Quilt as desired.

2. Cut the binding fabric into 2″ strips and sew together, end-to-end. Press the seams open. Press the binding in half along the width, wrong sides together, and use to finish the quilt (see page 62 for my binding method).

Get Inspired

Don't be afraid to make the cuts through the stacks really angular. When it comes time to join the blocks side-by-side, the shapes created will be more interesting the more you cut with abandon.

Variations

▷ Use a muted color pull but with a highly contrasting color for the center of the tiles. Rather than have the centers being all the same color, mix and match the blocks to create multi-colored centers. This works particularly well when coupled with a low-volume pull, as described above.

▷ Change the size and shape of your starting pieces. You can use smaller pieces for the stacks, just bear in mind that you will lose at least an inch once the two cuts are made. Smaller squares are great for showcasing a larger number of prints for a scrappier look. Elongated rectangles can create long, diamond shapes that are emphasized by the addition of the triangular snippets.

Quilting Notes

In a quilt of personal challenges, I wanted the quilting to be quite minimal. I'm an avid fan of dense quilting, the denser the better, yet for this I wanted to try something new. I was initially unsure of the large areas of unquilted fabric, but upon reflection, I found that these looping cursive e's add a calmness to the jagged piecing.

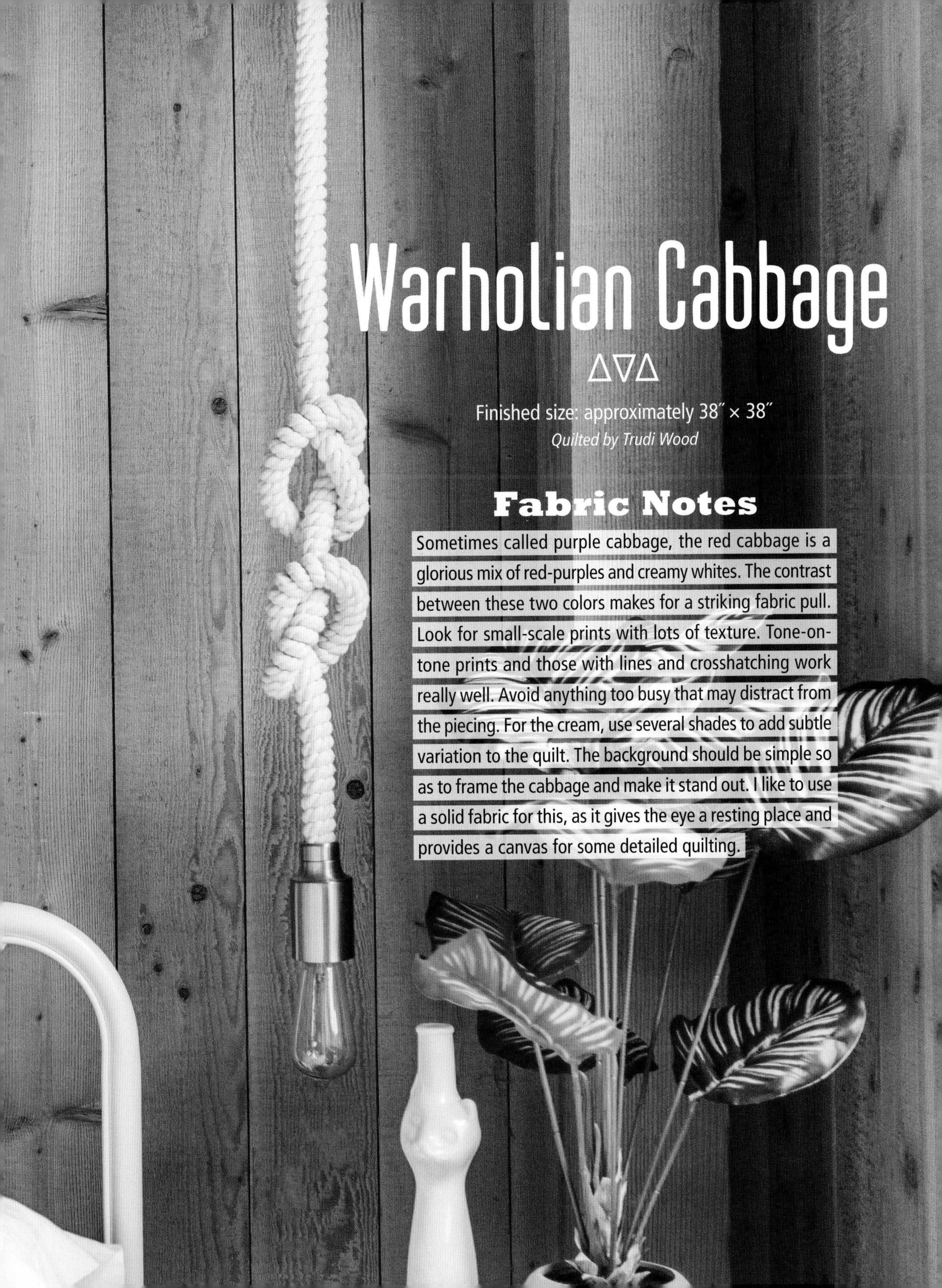

Warholian Cabbage

△▽△

Finished size: approximately 38″ × 38″

Quilted by Trudi Wood

Fabric Notes

Sometimes called purple cabbage, the red cabbage is a glorious mix of red-purples and creamy whites. The contrast between these two colors makes for a striking fabric pull. Look for small-scale prints with lots of texture. Tone-on-tone prints and those with lines and crosshatching work really well. Avoid anything too busy that may distract from the piecing. For the cream, use several shades to add subtle variation to the quilt. The background should be simple so as to frame the cabbage and make it stand out. I like to use a solid fabric for this, as it gives the eye a resting place and provides a canvas for some detailed quilting.

When I started quilting, never could I have imagined that vegetables would play such a prominent part in my creative practice. Let's be honest, it's definitely one of the stranger sources of inspiration! But vegetables have done more than inspire me to make a quilt or two. I wouldn't be writing these words were it not for the humble leek, so it feels right that vegetables should have a special mention.

I thought hard about which vegetable to include. In the end, the clear winner was cabbage. I remember my very first block based on this most beloved of Brassica. Its creation was purely guess work; an experiment without certainty of success. Perseverance and excitement kept me going until I finished the block. That instant then, having taken an idea and realized it in fabric, was the brightest of lightbulb moments.

I've taught classes to the most traditional of quilters, who soon lose themselves in the spontaneity of the technique. Don't be disheartened if yours doesn't look exactly like mine.

Practice joining slabs and make a smaller test block before embarking on a full-sized quilt. Once you're confident with the construction, the only limit is your imagination!

MATERIALS

AN ASSORTMENT OF PURPLE FABRICS: fat eights, totaling approximately 1½ yards

AN ASSORTMENT OF CREAM FABRICS: fat eights, totaling approximately 1 yard

Larger **PURPLE SCRAPS**

Larger **CREAM SCRAPS**

BACKGROUND FABRIC: approximately 1 yard

BATTING: at least 4″ wider and 4″ longer than your finished quilt top

BACKING FABRIC: at least 4″ wider and 4″ longer than your finished quilt top

BINDING FABRIC: approximately ⅓ yard

Piecing the Cabbage

1. Along the 21″ edges, cut the purple fabric into a variety of strips, from ¾″ to 1½″ wide. Set aside one cream fat eighth for the cabbage core and cut the rest into a variety of strips, from ¾″ to 1″ wide.

2. From a variety of the wider purple and cream scraps, use the triangle technique (see page 50), to make 8-10 triangle units for the core. My triangle units finished at approximately 2″ × 5″ to 3″ × 5″. Join the triangle units to make 2 approximately 21″ long strips.

3. Cut the remaining cream fabric into 2 strips and attach one to the base of each triangle strip from Step 2 to create two core sections.

4. On a design wall or similar large surface, mark an area approximately 40″ square to define the finished size. Using the photograph of the finished quilt on the next page for reference, place the 2 core sections vertically beside each other within the center of the marked area. Starting at the outside edge of one core section, use tape to roughly mark out your cabbage shape. Surround the entire cabbage with background fabric or have some edges fall outside the perimeter of the quilt top. This establishes the final cabbage shape and background.

5. Using the slab technique (see page 44) and the remaining strips, make around 10-12 large slabs. Don't worry about the finished size at this stage, just make sure there is a good variety of fabrics in each.

6. The cabbage is pieced in two halves. Working from one half of the core out to the side first, piece your slabs filling in that side. Be sure to alternate the direction of the strips so they appear random. Continue to work upward to the upper edge of the quilt. Use the slab offcuts to fill in the smaller areas at different angles, as desired. It won't matter if some of the triangle points of the core are cut off during this process, but do make sure the slabs extend past the marked perimeter so that the cabbage can be shaped a bit more later on.

7. Once one side is filled up to the taped cabbage outline, repeat for the other half. Work from the core first and then up. Consider cutting into your slabs to add a cream insert to break up the piecing even further. The goal is to create angular sections within the cabbage shape.

8. Once both halves of the cabbage are complete, straighten up the edges and sew the halves together or cut a freehand curve and join the halves that way.

Completing the Quilt Top

Use an erasable fabric marker to mark the perimeter of the cabbage and use the ring technique (see page 42) to add wide pieces of background fabric as needed. Return the quilt top to the perimeter guide periodically to check the coverage. Don't square up the quilt until after it has been quilted. See page 74 for Finishing instructions.

Get Inspired

Warholian Cabbage has perhaps the loosest construction of all the quilts in this book and can be somewhat intimidating the first time you look at it. Don't let how liberated it is put you off from attempting your own. There is a structure there, which can be easily adapted to suit the units you have made. Approach each step with confidence and remember that your cabbage will never look exactly like anyone else's.

Variations

▷ Use green or cream fabrics to mimic different cabbage varieties. Combine these to create a Warholian pop art quilt.

▷ Make smaller blocks and piece them together using the jigsaw method (see page 54).

▷ Use a brown or earth-colored background to give a planted field look.

▷ Go really, really big and create a king-sized cabbage. Adjust the size of the triangle units and make the slabs with wider and longer strips.

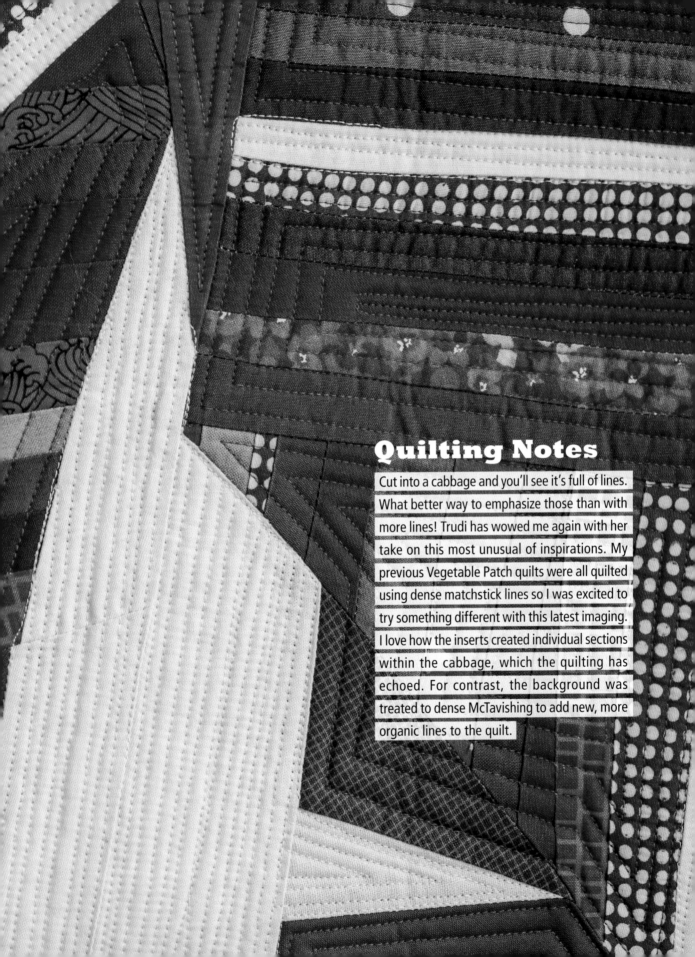

Quilting Notes

Cut into a cabbage and you'll see it's full of lines. What better way to emphasize those than with more lines! Trudi has wowed me again with her take on this most unusual of inspirations. My previous Vegetable Patch quilts were all quilted using dense matchstick lines so I was excited to try something different with this latest imaging. I love how the inserts created individual sections within the cabbage, which the quilting has echoed. For contrast, the background was treated to dense McTavishing to add new, more organic lines to the quilt.

きんつぎ
Kintsugi
△▽

Finished size: approximately 50″ × 50″

Fabric Notes

For my background fabrics, I took inspiration from examples of ancient Japanese pottery. The neutral tones work well as a background to the contrasting inserts. Using both solids and small-scale prints will add variation to the quilt without overwhelming it. You want the focus to be on the inserts, so avoid anything too busy. Nowadays, quilters have an abundance of choice when it comes to fabric, so look for something special for the inserts. I've used fabrics woven with metallic threads, but printed fabrics would work just as well. Use snippets of busier, large-scale prints to fill in gaps and add contrasting pops of color.

Kintsugi, or kintsukuroi, is a Japanese technique for mending broken pottery, translated as "golden joinery" or "golden repair." The cracks in the ceramics are repaired using a lacquer laced with powdered gold, creating metallic seams across the surface of the object. Often, gaps are filled with pieces of other ceramics to add further interest. There are reports of people throughout the centuries intentionally breaking items so that they could be repaired in this way, believing that the object becomes all the more beautiful for having been broken. The history is recognized and the repair, rather than being disguised, becomes a focal point.

I was so inspired when I first learned about this ancient art. I've always believed in taking risks in my quilt making, exploring new territory with excitement and eagerness. If ever I make a "mistake" and something doesn't turn out quite as expected, I use that as an opportunity. The "mistake" becomes part of the quilt's history, revitalizes it and helps it become something better than it would have been. Kintsugi embodies many Japanese beliefs — the acceptance of change, finding beauty in the flawed, and regretting waste — all of which are inherent in liberated sewing.

BACKGROUND: 6-8 fabrics, totaling approximately 3½ yards

METALLIC INSERT FABRICS: totaling approximately 1 yard, (4) ¼ yard cuts work best

Scraps of **CONTRASTING FABRICS**

BATTING: at least 4″ wider and 4″ longer than your finished quilt top

BACKING FABRIC: at least 4″ wider and 4″ longer than your finished quilt top

BINDING FABRIC: approximately ½ yard

To add a contrast piece, use the background piece as a template to cut the shape from the contrast fabric and use it in place of the background piece. Be sure to add more contrasting pieces to some of your blocks than you do to others. This will add variation to the quilt.

Piecing the Blocks

1. From the background fabrics, cut 25 approximately 14″ squares. These don't have to be exactly square, so feel free to use scissors.

2. Cut the insert fabrics into strips from ¾″ - 1″ wide across the WOF.

3. Use a rotary cutter to make several cuts through a background square. The goal is to add an insert strip between each cut. Using the photograph of the finished quilt on the next page as a guide, start by making a cut from one edge of the square to the other. Subcut these sections, keeping the cut pieces in place on the cutting mat. Aim to make about 5 to 8 cuts, avoiding making any of the pieces too small.

4. From a strip of insert fabric, cut pieces a bit longer than the cuts from Step 3 in the background square. Allow an overhang at each end of around ¼″, as described in the insert technique (see page 39).

5. Sew the insert strips to the background pieces, beginning with the smallest insert lengths first or working in reverse order across the unit to rebuild the block. Press after each insert addition.

6. Repeat Steps 3-5 for the remaining squares of background fabric, making sure to vary the direction of your cuts.

7. Once all 25 blocks are pieced, press well and trim each to a 10½″ square.

Completing the Quilt Top

Arrange the 10½″ blocks into a 5 × 5 grid. Once you are happy with the arrangement, sew the blocks together into rows, pressing the seams of the different rows in alternate directions to allow them to interlock. Sew the rows together to complete the quilt top.

Finishing

See page 74 for Finishing instructions.

Get Inspired

As you sew the inserts and the background together, you may need to trim some of the edges straight before sewing them to other pieces.

Variations

▷ I used a number of background fabrics to give the look of various pieces of pottery joined together. For a simpler look, use the same background fabric in all your blocks. Be sure to choose a fabric that contrasts with the insert fabric adjoining it. Similarly, rather than using different metallic fabrics, choose only one for a more cohesive look.

▷ Take a larger piece of background fabric and fill it with inserts to make a slab. Use the ring technique (see page 42) to add contrasting fabric to one or two sides. This focuses the attention on a single piece of repaired pottery and makes for a modern, striking design.

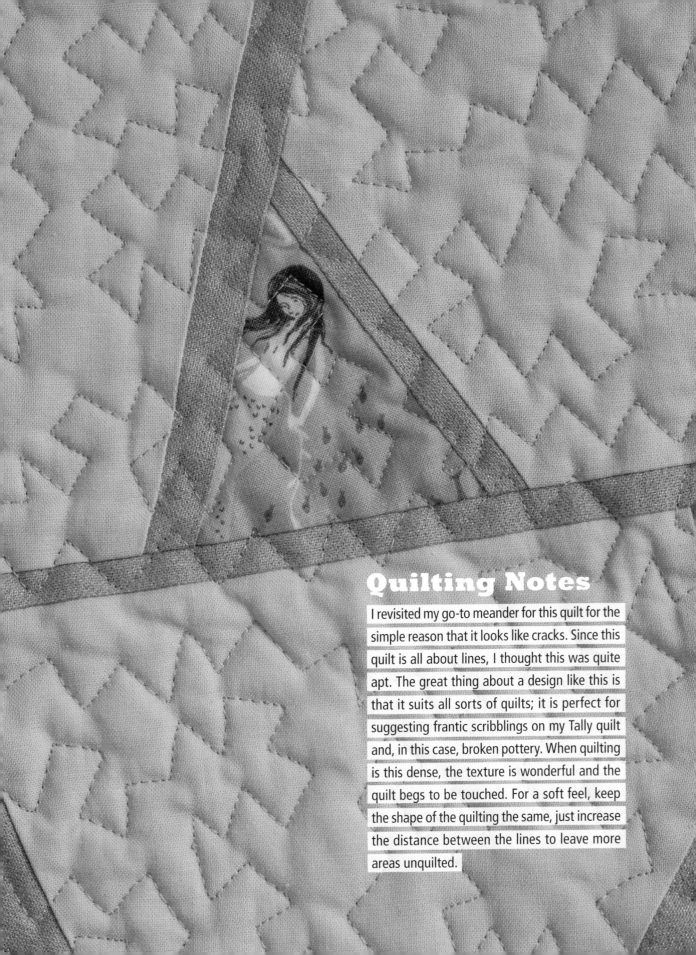

Quilting Notes

I revisited my go-to meander for this quilt for the simple reason that it looks like cracks. Since this quilt is all about lines, I thought this was quite apt. The great thing about a design like this is that it suits all sorts of quilts; it is perfect for suggesting frantic scribblings on my Tally quilt and, in this case, broken pottery. When quilting is this dense, the texture is wonderful and the quilt begs to be touched. For a soft feel, keep the shape of the quilting the same, just increase the distance between the lines to leave more areas unquilted.

After Seurat

△

Finished size: approximately 48″ × 48″

Fabric Notes

While the piecing of this quilt is inspired by pointillism, my chosen colors came from an image I saw on Instagram of hundreds of streamers fluttering in the wind. As in Drunken Tiles, I kept to an almost entirely solid pull, using a pink palette to create a range of tones from lightest shell to saturated and shocking. I added a complementary trio of ochre tones to break up the pink and create secondary shapes within the composition. The dissecting line was the perfect place to showcase a favorite print.

Whenever I'm on holiday, I always seek out three things: fabric shops, natural history museums and art galleries. If I hadn't become so enamored with quilting, I'd fill my time by collecting fossils and painting. I love impressionism, surrealism, and anything that moves beyond the traditional. The inspiration for this quilt came from the pointillist movement — a technique in which small, distinct dots of color are applied in patterns to form an image — specifically, the works of French artist Georges-Pierre Seurat, who moved away from the spontaneity of impressionism to develop a much more structured style.

Now, I imagine you're all thinking: "Isn't spontaneity at the heart of improv quilting?" To which I reply: "Yes, it is!" The blocks of this quilt are made using the stack technique and are still improv at heart. Nothing has changed there. The structure comes from the grouping of colors and using them to create lines and shapes within the quilt. Like in pointillist works of art, I wanted the quilt to showcase small units of color, similar to the way dots of paint are used to create pattern. A simple, bold line dissects my quilt from top to bottom, though you can use the stack technique to create all sorts of shapes; words, trees, even people.

Piecing the Units

MATERIALS

MAIN COLORS: 8-10 fat quarters

COMPLEMENTARY COLORS: 2-4 fat quarters

CONTRASTING COLOR: 1 fat quarter (optional)

BATTING: at least 4″ wider and 4″ longer than your finished quilt top

BACKING FABRIC: at least 4″ wider and 4″ longer than your finished quilt top

BINDING FABRIC: approximately ⅓ yard

1. Cut each fat quarter into 12 approximately 5½″ squares. These don't have to be exactly square so feel free to use scissors for this step.

2. The quilt is constructed from (144) 4-patch units, combined into 12 rows of 12 units each. There are no hard and fast rules for how to combine your fabrics. To achieve a gradation of color, arrange the main fabrics in order of value and number them in ascending order. For the first and second row, use the stack technique (see page 46) to create 4-patch units from fabrics 1, 2 , 3 and 4. For the third and fourth rows, use fabrics 3, 4, 5 and 6. Continue in this way, introducing the complementary colors from row 5 onward. Another option is to combine the various units randomly and group colors together when arranging the quilt top.

3. To add shape or movement, switch out one of the fabrics in a stack for a piece of contrasting fabric. I recommend using graph paper to plot the course of the desired shape. This will make it easier to determine exactly how many units of the contrast fabric are required. More than one piece of the fabric may need to be added to a unit to create a bend. Refer to the photograph of the finished quilt on the next page to see how I have used these in my version. My line was inspired by the streamers that contributed to the color scheme. Feel free to create a unique shape using this method.

4. Once all of the 4-patch units are assembled, trim each to 4½″ square.

Completing the Quilt Top

1. Arrange the units, closely following any guides or drawings you may have made. I recommend taking a photograph of the finished arrangement before assembling, to act as a reference should any of the units on a design wall accidentally move out of position.

2. Sew the units of the first row together. I recommend sewing six larger 4-patch blocks together first, then joining these to complete the row. When sewing the rows, press the seams of the different rows in alternate directions to allow the seams to interlock. Sew the rows together and press to complete the quilt top.

Finishing

Follow the Finishing instructions on page 74.

Get Inspired

When arranging the units into rows, take a few from the row above and move them into the current row to make the color changes less rigid and blend them into each other more.

Variations

▷ Make the starting squares smaller to achieve even more detailed compositions by combining smaller units and more colors.

▷ Use a pixilating app or website to turn any image or photograph into a quilt design. Note the number of different fabrics needed and calculate the number of unit combinations needed, simplifying if necessary. This more adventurous approach will require a little more forethought, so use graph paper to keep track of the units.

▷ Use various shades of black, white, and gray fabric for a monochromatic look.

Quilting Notes

As I was piecing this quilt, the first units I made were the softer pink ones at the bottom. I was reminded of pearls and the pearlescence inside clam shells. With that in mind, there was really only one choice when it came to the quilting design. I think After Seurat is the quilt that draws inspiration from the most sources: a nineteenth-century painter for the piecing, carnival streamers for the fabric pull, and a mollusk for the quilting. Quite the eclectic mix!

Topography

△▽△

Finished size: approximately 30″ × 33″

Fabric Notes

I based my palette on older geographical survey maps and photographs I came across during my research, though you could use any color story for this quilt. Various shades of gray give the look of a black-and-white photograph, high in contrast and perfect for suggesting the lines that make up the landscape. During my time at university, I was a fan of using bright whites and deep blacks in my photographs and would often intentionally burn out areas when in the darkroom. This fabric pull pays homage to those days of photographic experimentation.

From this book's earliest origins, I knew I wanted to feature a quilt that could illustrate all the various improvised techniques. I had lines and patterns on the brain and began to look at old maps and aerial photographs of towns and villages. I came to see they were full of gentle curves, crossed lines, and slabs of color — perfect inspiration for an improv quilter. Topography is the result of that inspiration. Think of this quilt as a way to take all you've learned and apply it to a single project. It is the most liberated project in this book, and as such, you'll find few specific instructions or variations. Since there are no rules in this imaginary landscape, it's perfect for showcasing your favorite techniques. Feel free to add larger fields of color, a wilder river, or more houses to accommodate a bustling population.

Quilting Notes

The curving, echoing lines of topographical maps were really the only choice for this quilt. Like the quilt itself, this is a design you can have real fun with. You can echo for as long as you like, then throw in an unexpected bump or turn. Good basting will set you up for success with this design, as will ensuring you leave enough room to echo back out. Be sure to consider scale too. Owing to the small size of my finished top, my lines are quite close together. If you are making a larger quilt, you can increase the spacing between the lines.

Piecing the Quilt Top

I found it easiest to approach this quilt with an initial reference image. Search the library or the internet for an aerial image to use as inspiration. Using the various techniques (see pages 36-53) and my inspiration image as a guide, make a number of units. Make several slabs with smaller inserts to suggest houses and dwellings. Join wide strips of fabric then subcut into thinner strips. The stack technique is perfect for making fields, using both straight and curved seams. My advice is to make a wide range of units of various sizes, so that you have plenty of options when it comes to joining them all together.

Once you've sewn enough units for your chosen image, begin to arrange them on a design wall or floor. At this stage, individual components will be a mix of sizes and the edges may be curved or straight. Refer back to your inspirational image as a guide to joining the pieces. Use the jigsaw method (see page 54) to piece the units together, using both straight and curved seams. Add further interest to the quilt by using the insert technique to suggest rivers, roads and hedgerows. What's important to remember is that you're looking to achieve a feeling of a topographical map rather than replicate it exactly.

Finishing

Follow the instruction on page 74 for Finishing.

Get Inspired

This one is simple. Just let loose and have fun creating a fabric landscape! I haven't suggested any variations for this quilt as it can already be made in so many different ways. Take inspiration from my quilt but don't try to replicate it. It's far easier, and more enjoyable, to let the fabric and the way you cut it, guide you.

AFTERWORD: A QUILT OF TWO HALVES

WHENEVER I HEAR the phrase "blood, sweat and tears," I have to admit to rolling my eyes. It likens something as simple as unpacking groceries to scaling Everest in deepest winter. I've heard it mentioned in the context of making a quilt too, which made me think that whoever the quilter was, they must have been doing something wrong.

When I began the process of writing this book, I naïvely thought I was prepared. After graduating from art school, I lived in Paris, proudly embracing every cliché. I dabbled in writing, even acquiring a secondhand typewriter, which I would prop up on a café's terrace table and bash at the keys. When you're writing a book sans publisher, it's all Hemingway-esque, Moleskine notepads and inspirational strolls in the rain. When you have deadlines and a contractual obligation, it turns out, it's quite stressful!

So, I did sweat as I raced to get everything done in time. There was even blood, thanks to an unfortunate combination of a new rotary cutter blade and a slip of the hand. The tears, however, were something entirely unexpected.

As you may have learned by now, improvised sewing relies on an acceptance of change. Units need to be re-sewn, re-trimmed, or perhaps scrapped entirely. When planning the quilts for this book, I was excited to expand the technique used in the blocks of my Vegetable Patch quilts by upscaling a block to a much larger version. It was then that How to Age a Tree was born.

Construction began with enthusiastic vigor. Usually the creative process for me is a series of highs and lows. It starts with me thinking "this is awesome" before progressing to "this is tricky, this is rubbish and I'm rubbish" before I settle on "this might be okay." Never had this mantra been truer than when I was making How to Age a Tree. I even pretended not to notice the fullness that the quilt top was taking on after each new ring addition, until reaching a point where it could no longer be ignored. Enter Trudi Wood, quilter extraordinaire. We exchanged photographs and messages; me detailing my concerns and she doing her best to appease them. After these comforting words, I hoped all would be fine and the top could and would be quilted into submission. As it turned out, it couldn't be, and that's when the tears flowed.

Upon closer inspection, Trudi realized how much fullness there really was, like nothing she'd ever encountered in her years of quilting. We decided to make a crack in the trunk, and I have her to thank for that bold addition. But, it still would not lie flat. I was running out of time and didn't know what to do. A brainstorming session with my close friend Nydia concluded with the suggestion of remaking the quilt in a quilt-as-you-go style, but I couldn't. This quilt had to be in the book.

"Shall I just cut the bloody thing in half?" I suggested in a moment of desperation.

Suddenly, I had a renewed enthusiasm for the quilt. My mind began to race. I wasn't upset any more. I was excited. When it comes to quilt design, I'm no computer wizard, preferring graph paper and an HB pencil. I took an image of the quilt on my iPhone and used notes to block out half the quilt. It was amateurish, but it gave me an idea, a seed, "kindling for further exploration." Here I was, crying over a quilt, when the answer was there all along. "What may be perceived as an obstacle can, in improv, be an opportunity for creative expression." My own words. Art imitating life.

The rest happened quickly. Trudi, in what I can only imagine was one of the most daring and nerve-racking things she's ever had to do to a customer's quilt, literally cut my quilt in half. There was no going back now. The only way out was through. We formulated a quilting plan: wood grain for the tree in an amber, resin-like color and echoing for the lines, with "ghost

rings" for the missing slice of trunk. When the quilt was returned to me, I was blown away. It was perfect. The tears, the stress and the bitter disappointment were all forgotten when I saw this newly realized work, which is now one of my favorite quilts (or two of them) in the book.

The tale of the quilt of two halves is a cautionary one, reminding us there is always a choice, a way to make the best of what at first may seem like a bad situation. Cry if you have to. Think it over, but don't overthink it. Be bold, be brave, and inspire your own improv!

ACKNOWLEDGMENTS

AFTER COUNTLESS BOBBINS, a dozen thread colors, two bottles of Flatter, Ru Paul on repeat, enough coffee to rival Brazil and a sewing room that looks like a firework factory shared space with a fabric shop, we've reached the acknowledgments page. I found writing a book to be a lonely process. I was in my head a lot, thinking things out, making lists of lists and mentally racing towards so many deadlines. It was all togther a fun, exhilarating, and exhausting process, made both possible and bearable by the love and support of friends and family.

Firstly, to Barri, my soul mate and my best friend: You put up with my moaning and mess, turning a blind eye to the threads that clung to the carpets, the sofa, the dressing gowns, and the dog. You were a bringer of coffee and a maker of meals during the weeks and months of quilt construction and the best dog dad Samuel could wish for. While you may not fully understand this world of fabric and followers I live in, you embrace it nonetheless and allow me to flourish. For this, I thank you a thousand times over. Samuel: You snoring at my feet during the long days of sewing made the hours fly by. You deserve the longest walk and a roast chicken dinner.

Mother and Father: Many thanks for your support and interest in my endeavors over the years. They have been both numerous and varied, though I think this quilting thing is here to stay.

Grandmother: The fact that I wrote this book shows just how much I have to thank you for. My love of sewing was evident at an early age and wouldn't have bore fruit if not for your constant encouragement and support. You've helped me in so many other ways too. Remember those early mornings when we would work through lists of spelling words? Clearly, you knew then that such phrases as "Betty eats cakes and usually shares eggs" would put me in good stead whenever I had to spell "because."

To those who have supported me when this book was a mere idea, I thank you. Zaynub, Stephanie, and Jo: I miss you and running my mad ideas by you. Many past projects were made all the better by your open and honest feedback. Ben: This book is one of many we've discussed over cups of coffee and pints of beer, and possibly a sweet chilli chicken wrap. I'm glad to finally get one to the stage where you can actually hold it in your hands! Thanks for lending an ear whenever I needed it.

To Susanne and everyone at Lucky Spool Media: thank you for your faith in the project and for giving me the chance to fulfill a long-held ambition. I'm so excited to see how people embrace improv and shake up the way they sew. Together, I think we've made something really special.

To all at Page + Pixel: Thank you for making my book look as beautiful as you have. It was my dream to have How to Age a Tree photogrpahed amongst real redwoods and you made it a reality.

Lorna: You are one of my oldest and dearest friends. You selflessly gave up your time and for a brief moment, it was like we were back in art school, young and out-of-the-box thinking. There were no flowers in flames this time, but nonetheless, the resulting images of our collaboration make the book all-the-more special.

Nydia: I'm so glad we were able to connect at Glamp Stitchalot and forge the friendship that we have. I would not have made it through this process without you. We bounced ideas back and forth, talked fabric and thread, and made it through together. Your talent and creativity helped me when I was mired, pulling me out of many a rut via a virtual slap through the screen. You are kind, loving, and generous with your time. I look forward to many more oportunities to teach you all about tea.

Anyone who knows me will say that I'm a bit of a perfectionist and place heavy demands on myself in the pursuit of my craft. Entrusting someone else with my work takes a leap of faith, and one I'd take blindly when Trudi Wood is concerned. Trudi, you have taken my vision and added your own inspiring talent and creativity. Your quilting is far beyond anything I could have ever imagined, and my quilts are made better by being quilted by you. Here's to many more collaborations.

Ian: Your illustrations are perfect. You just got it and weren't put off by my vague and child-like scribblings. You nailed the translation from words to pictures. Keep doing what you do, because it's working.

An extra special thanks to Katy Jones, my quilt wife (sorry, Quilt Dad, but we'll have to share her). It feels like we've been friends for much longer than it's been, and I miss ~~sipping~~ guzzling gin with you in deepest North Wales. You believed in me when I came to you with crazy ideas (like quilts inspired by pizzas) and your support as editor of Quilt Now allowed me to share my passion for improv with an audience. I am eternally grateful.

Much appreciation to everyone at Bogod and Bernina UK, in particular to Howard, Richard, and Stephen, for their generosity in welcoming me into the Bernina community. And to Steph: You kept a secret better than I could. You're a kind and supportive soul who allows me to be the passenger. Thank you.

The quilts in this book were made with the support and generosity of many people within the quilting and sewing community. I would like to extend my extreme gratitude to Dashwood Studio, Higgs and Higgs, Lecien, Me+You, Oakshott, and Robert Kaufman for supplying fabric; to Aurifil for supplying thread; to Barnyarns for the notions and continued support; Soak for providing Flatter spray; and Lady Sew and Sew for the batting.

My love of quilting has taken me across the world and introduced me to so many kind and inspiring people. I'll be forever grateful that I've been given the opportunity to give back, in however small a way, and share my passion for improv with you all. A huge final thanks to you who are reading these words, and to the followers, commenters, and class takers. Your words and encouragement are so welcomed. To the improv toe-dippers and the dive-right-inners, I'm excited to see your interpretations of these techniques. As a promoter of the nontraditional, all I can ask is that people try, so without further delay, go forth and sew!

"Working in the liberated quilt making style is like taking a trip in a snowstorm. You can only see three feet in front of you, but you can make the whole trip that way."

—Gwen Marston, fibre artist and author